A YEAR
IN THE ART
OF A
PRIMARY
SCHOOL

Robert Clement and Elizabeth Tarr

Photographs by John Morton

NATIONAL SOCIETY FOR EDUCATION IN ART & DESIGN

ACKNOWLEDGEMENTS

We wish to thank the following for their various contributions towards the work of this book.

Annette Mason, Curriculum Leader for Art and Design at Thornbury Primary School, for her enthusiasm and expertise and for that love for her work that has been so instrumental towards making Art and Design central to the curriculum at Thornbury.

The teaching staff at Thornbury Primary School, 1988/89.

Fiona Banks, Alison Hurdle, Hilary Barratt, Lesley Knowlton, Sally Brimblecombe, Carol McQuire, Rebecca Buckle, Jan Marshall, Garry Cleasby, Judy Matthews, Hilary Creber, Wendy Pierce, Jackie Daw, Rebecca Taylor, Sue Goad, Julie Tyler, Mary Hatherley, Terry West, Jonathan Heywood, Sue Harmes

The children at Thornbury Primary School

The National Society for Education in Art and Design for providing us with the opportunity to present this work to the public.

The Members and Officers of Devon Education Committee who provide the framework and the resources for our work.

Bob Clement and Liz Tarr
August 1990

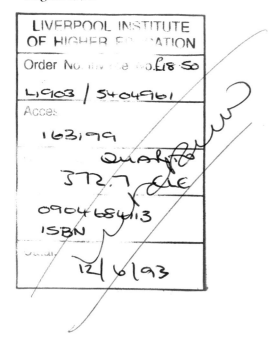

For David, Helen and Jane
For keeping us sane

CONTENTS

7. APPRAISAL AND ASSESSMENT

PART TWO

INTRODUCTION

8. AUTUMN TERM 1988 Aspects of Spiral One

9. SPRING TERM 1989 Aspects of Spiral Three

10. SUMMER TERM 1989 Aspects of Spiral Three

APPENDIX

Visual Reference and Resource Material used within the School in 1988/89

FOREWORD

'A Year in the Art of a Primary School' is not overly concerned with theoretical curriculum development. It is a carefully documented pragmatic account of the art and design work which actually took place in Thornbury Primary School, Devon, in the course of one academic year. It therefore provides an example of what can be done with thoughtful planning and with the commitment of dedicated teachers the majority of whom have not specialist art and design training.

The book is one in a series of publications of the *National Society for Education in Art and Design* that are intended to disseminate examples of good practice. The approach to art and design education revealed in the following pages is not slavishly meshed to National Curriculum attainment targets and programmes of study but it will be immediately apparent to the reader that a sensible correlation exists with the statutory Orders.

It is no accident that the thinking underpinning the work at Thornbury Primary School is in tune with new developments in art and design education – the co-authors have been closely in touch with recent initiatives and they are in an unrivalled position to share a wealth of relevant experience with classroom teachers.

The headteacher at Thornbury, Liz Tarr, MBE, served as a member of the School Examinations and Assessment Council from 1988 to 1991 and during her period of office she chaired the SEAC Art Committee.

Bob Clement, OBE, was the County Art Adviser for Devon from 1970 until his retirement in the Spring of 1992. Bob is a former chairman of the Schools Council Art Committee (1975-82), he served as secretary of the Association of Art Advisers (1973-76) and was chairman of the Society for Education through Art until its merger to form the NSEAD in 1984. He was President of the NSEAD in 1985. He was a leading member of the National Curriculum Art Working Group (1990-1991). Bob was also a key member of the team that devised the NSEAD publication 'Art, Craft and Design in the Primary School' (1987) and he is the author of 'The Art Teacher's Handbook' (1986).

I confidently predict that this book will continue to provide valuable ideas and insights to inspire primary art co-ordinators and classroom teachers long after the statutory Order for Art has been buried under a layer of dust on staffroom bookshelves.

John Steers
General Secretary, NSEAD
September 1992

PART ONE

INTRODUCTION

Thornbury Primary School in Plymouth was opened in 1978. It sits amongst a vast sprawl of modern, mainly local authority housing on the Northern edge of the City. It was built to accommodate 560 children and as a school of this size can be intimidating to young children, every effort has been made to create an environment that is both welcoming and comfortable. This is particularly important because the school has its fair share of the complex social problems that may be found in any large city.

Liz Tarr opened the school with a small nucleus of staff and has had that good fortune to start a new school 'from scratch'. She came to the school with a rich experience in early years teaching, a love of mathematics and some interest in art, craft and design. The way in which the Thornbury curriculum has evolved and the central part that the visual arts have played in its development are described in some detail in Chapter Two.

From its very beginning, there was a strong commitment within the school to teach art, craft and design as valuable and discrete areas of experience for all children. As the school has developed and the curriculum has been shaped, Liz Tarr and her colleagues have come to see how the arts may be taught and used not just for their own intrinsic value, but as positive agents in children's learning across the curriculum.

In this development the school has been well- supported by its curriculum leaders for art and design, Helen Stokes, who is now Headteacher of Chaddlewood Infant School and Annette Mason, the present Deputy Headteacher.

Both teachers were quick to become involved with the policy of school- based in-service work, recognising that with well over 500 children and with over 20 staff, there was no place for a curriculum leader who simply led by example and looked after the displays of children's work in the entrance foyer. Consequently, at Thornbury, there has been a strong commitment to school-based in-service work to support the teaching of the visual arts across the school and a variety of team teaching and management strategies developed to support the emergence of a coherent programme of work in art and design.

The development of work at the school has been continuously influenced by the Devon County Advisory Team for Art and Design, led by Bob Clement. This team, whilst giving encouragement and support, has always asked the right questions at the wrong time!

o 'The observed drawing is very good – but have you thought about using other kinds of drawing?'

o 'How can you use drawing in support of work in ceramics?'

o 'What is the difference between illustrating a topic and extending and enriching it through art and design?'

This kind of questioning has helped the teachers to analyse their work and build upon their achievements.

There is within the school a very real commitment to a curriculum that is based on real experience and real learning. This is exemplified in the way that children's learning in all subjects is based upon a progression from investigation of their own immediate world towards an understanding of their place within the larger community of the school, the local environment, the city and the world beyond Devon.

It is evident that work in art and design can play a very significant part in support of any curriculum which is so focused upon helping children to make sense of the world in which they live and in which real investigation and real learning play such an important part.

This book is primarily a description of the way that art and design has been taught and used in one academic year in the life of a good primary school. For the children in the school it is just another year in which they have been encouraged to enjoy their learning and have been given a rich variety of experiences and challenges in all aspects of their school work.

For the teaching staff, 1988-89 – the period surveyed in this book – was a momentous year in which they were challenged by the emergence and demands of the new national curriculum and its assessment. Art & Design and Technology are part of the new National Curriculum: at Thornbury, they are richly embedded in the work of the school and are used as essential ingredients in children's learning.

The authors hope that this description of art, craft and design activities in the work of one school in one academic year, will help other teachers to see how they might develop their teaching in this area of the curriculum more effectively. In particular, it should help teachers to reinforce and extend children's learning beyond their making of images and artefacts for their own sake, into a deeper understanding of the world in which they live.

Our experience suggests that it is comparatively easy to structure children's learning in such a way that they may be enabled to produce pleasing and attractive images. You can 'programme' children to make well-observed drawings or attractive objects to take home to their parents. It is much more of a challenge to find ways to enable children to use art and design purposefully and to be educated through the making of art.

'A Year in the Art of a Primary School' is presented in two sections. The first part deals with the basic principles that underpin both the work of Thornbury

Fig. 1.1. Children from Year 2 drawing in the school grounds

Fig. 1.2. Year 2 drawing of school building and plants. Fibre tip pen

Primary School and its approach to the teaching of art, craft and design.

○ What is the place and purpose of the subject?
○ How is it organised and resourced?
○ What structure and sequence supports its work?
○ How are the different aspects of Art and Design taught and used?

The second part consists of detailed descriptions of a number of cross-curriculum projects that have been undertaken in the school. These will illustrate and explain the way that work in art and design may be used across the primary age range and in support of a variety of cross-curricular themes.

These descriptions should help you to see that the good teaching of art and design will enrich children's learning in language, in the humanities, in environmental studies and in science and technology.

Where the arts are taught in splendid isolation, for their own sake and regardless of the needs of children in the real world they move inevitably to the periphery of the primary school curriculum.

THE THORNBURY CURRICULUM

2.1. GENERAL PRINCIPLES

The purpose of this chapter is to set succeeding chapters in the context of the particular aims and ethos of Thornbury Primary School.

The overall aim of the school is to make every child confident in his or her ability within a well-structured and happy environment. Our purpose is to give every child 'a rage to learn' and in our present climate of change this requires the development of a wide range of strategies to keep children highly motivated.

We believe that the education of a child is a partnership between the child, the parents and the school. Confidence, trust and understanding have to be the basic foundation of any partnership if it is to succeed. We give a high profile to our home and school programme through which parents are encouraged to take an active part in their children's education. There is a strong parent education programme which begins before the child enters the school and which helps parents to understand the school curriculum and its policy throughout their children's schooling. This 'open door' philosophy helps the school to flourish within the community.

The school is a team-teaching cooperative. It has an environment where teachers are encouraged to develop, share and practise their personal skills. This stems from the belief that all primary school teachers cannot be good at everything and that as professionals we can all learn from each other in a non-hierarchal way. All curriculum policies have been – and still are – formulated by all the staff working together so that everyone becomes party to the decision-making process and is thus involved in the constantly evolving philosophy of the school. We think it is important to offer a rich pattern of education to support and extend the work of the core subjects: an education that has breadth, depth, relevance, coherence, progression and differentiation. We have to consider fully the needs of every child and the potential contained within his or her individual talents and difficulties. We believe that all children should be extended through a variety of experiences and a range of learning methods.

In the early years of this school we had to work hard to establish the belief that if we wanted a curriculum of quality and richness then 'The Arts' had to be a part of our daily bread and butter and not a decorative afterthought. All the staff believe that the arts provide a rich vehicle for exploring all areas of the curriculum. The arts encourage and enable children to have an understanding of the world in which they live and those others who share this world with them. Teaching through the arts encourages children to look, think, feel and respond to a wide range of experiences, starting with themselves and their families when they are in the younger egocentric stage, and moving out to the wider community and other cultures as they move through the school. This broadening of the teachers' view of the arts and how they might be used in the school was developed through systematic school based in-service work reinforced by the success that teachers experienced when they used the arts as a starting point to work across the curriculum.

The second priority is to teach through a thematic approach so that children experience the wholeness of their curriculum. Each project contains whatever fits naturally to the understanding of the theme. Therefore curriculum balance is maintained across the year rather than from week to week or term by term. The agreed balance informs our priorities for the work. This approach requires very careful record keeping of the children's work so that each theme both builds upon skills already learnt and supports and extends the children's experiences. Some of the work of the school such as phonics, handwriting, reading, PE and games needs its own independent structure. Thematic maths needs to be supported by a structured maths teaching programme.

To support our belief in the importance of real and relevant experiences the curriculum is based upon the development of skills and concepts. The staff work to seven key concepts; similarity and difference, cause and effect, changes, communication, stewardship, power, conflict and consensus. Not all of these apply to each theme but some such as similarity and difference nearly always appear.

Thematic work allows one area of the curriculum to fertilise another but that in turn requires teachers to understand the essence of each subject area and be able to identify which skills and concepts are established through discussion and debate, reinforced through experience and practice and detailed in the schools policy documents for each area of the curriculum.

The curriculum at Thornbury is divided into manageable units. For identification and planning purposes it is divided into six broad areas.

LANGUAGE DEVELOPMENT

This is the umbrella of the curriculum. It encompasses talking and listening, reading and writing.

THE ARTS

Drama, dance, music, art and design, literature, poetry, media studies.

THE HUMANITIES

History, geography, religious education, personal social and moral development.

SCIENCE

Physical science, environmental science and health education.

MATHEMATICS

Computation, problem solving, mental agility and thematic work.

NON-THEMATIC WORK

Which has its own sequence and which needs adhering to as in physical education and games, spelling, phonics, handwriting.

Problem-solving and technology are used across all areas of the curriculum as recently endorsed by the National Curriculum programmes of study in technology and design. Information technology is an inherent part of the whole process.

When choosing a theme the main aim is that it should be relevant to the children concerned and motivate their enthusiasm for learning as well as providing opportunities for teaching the necessary skills and concepts. It is now additionally important that any Attainment Targets laid down by the National Curriculum are properly covered and recorded.

2.2. REAL EXPERIENCE AND REAL LEARNING

Perhaps the best way to show how policy works in practice is to offer four case studies as illustrations. These studies took place with different age groups, for different lengths of time and with different starting points. They show the links between art and design and other areas of the curriculum. All the children are in mixed ability classes.

These four case studies are forerunners to the more detailed themes in the second part of this book. The studies are concerned respectively with design and technology, history, the environment and fiction.

CASE STUDY 1
AN INDUSTRY PROJECT
AGE: 10/11 YEARS
TIME: 5 WEEKS
DESIGN AND TECHNOLOGY BASED

An important part of childrens's education is to make them aware that they have stewardship for the world around them. They have a responsibility to look after their environment and where better to start than their own school grounds.

The aim of this project was to involve children in

planning their own environment and to involve them in the problem of resourcing. The teachers also wanted to make the children aware of the world of work.

The children each began by designing and making a ceramic plaque. They collected leaves and flowers from the hedgerow in the school grounds and made careful studies of these in drawings and water colours. These studies were used as the basis for designing the plaques which were built in clay using slab and relief decoration techniques. While the plaques were going through the process of drying and firing, the children began to design and make the packaging for them. At the same time another group undertook the monotonous task of covering with hessian the blocks on which the plaques were to be mounted; these children had previously been involved with a really creative aspect of the work. A wide range of mathematical tasks were undertaken to design the packaging, to estimate the cost of manufacture and to decide upon the price of the plaques in order to make 'a reasonable profit'. This last statement generated interesting discussions about the moral issues of profit.

As part of the project they contacted by letter and by telephone local firms and the bank to seek advice about advertising, packaging and marketing. They looked at how personnel are appointed to firms, wrote job descriptions, short-listed suitable candidates, interviewed and appointed the team to lead their sales campaign. Finally they sold 120 plaques at the School Fayre and used the profits to put into action part of their plan to introduce a pond, meadow, and Devon hedgerow into the school grounds.

During this project the children learnt a lot of academic facts but more than this, experienced a whole range of attitudes and values that are important to everyday life.

CASE STUDY 2
THE ARMADA EXPERIENCE
AGE: 9/10 YEARS
TIME: WHOLE SUMMER TERM
HISTORY BASED

While Plymouth was celebrating the 250th anniversary of the Armada those teachers working with years 5 and 6 took the opportunity to ask of the children 'What do you think Plymouth was like 250 years ago?' The project started at the end of the Spring term with the teachers asking the children to arrive on the first day of the Summer term in Elizabethan costume. A letter was sent to parents explaining the purpose of the project and illustrating how simple costumes could be put together. The staff and children arrived on the first day of term suitably attired and 'Drake', a local character, arrived to tell the children about Plymouth in his time. The music teacher introduced the children to some Elizabethan music and dances and so the 'aura' was set.

During the course of the first week the children

visited the city centre to seek clues to the past and identify differences between what is left of the Elizabethan city and Plymouth today. During the term they studied the history of the Armada through primary and secondary evidence. This culminated in them designing and building a living museum which spread across seven class bases – each one reflecting a different aspect of Elizabethan life and times: the village green, a fisherman's cottage, an Elizabethan street, a kitchen, a harbour, a long room and a theatre. This involved all the staff in removing furniture, re-allocating teaching space into suitable workshops and setting these up accordingly – a mammoth piece of work but well worth it.

Parents became very involved in helping to make a wide variety of more complex costumes. The living museum was opened to the public towards the end of the term and the children re-enacted the life of the times working in a variety of settings on different days to make them aware that differences in homes and working life depended very much upon people's circumstances. Alongside this, a sixth group turned an outside quadrangle into an Elizabethan knot garden, researching all the information they needed by visiting gardens of the period and through reference books. The whole project was a dynamic inter-active experience for children, staff and parents.

To carry out a project of this dimension the work had to be planned well before the end of the previous term because of the implications for resourcing and timetabling. All the work was carefully detailed week by week to enable children to have the right balance and variety of experiences. The quality of their writing in a variety of modes was exceptional as was the art, craft and technology. The children came to a real understanding of an important part of the history of their community through engaging in this real and relevant way with times past.

CASE STUDY 3
COMPARISON OF INDUSTRIAL AND RURAL
LANDSCAPE
AGE: 9 YEARS
TIME: 4 WEEKS
ENVIRONMENT BASED

This project was specifically planned to enable the children to experience similarities and differences of landscapes.

The project started with a visit to the Royal Albert Museum in Exeter to see the touring exhibition of the work of L S Lowry. In the exhibition, the children worked on a number of tasks (Fig 3.12 page 19) and followed this up with a great deal of critical studies work paying particular attention to what Lowry's work told them about life in a city in the north of England. They then compared Lowry's images with light industry on the Thornbury estate and tried to illustrate the similarities and differences through drawing, painting and writing. The third week of the project was taken up with a visit to a residential centre in the rural heart of North Devon where they

had the opportunity to observe the similarities and differences between rural and industrial landscapes. They reached conclusions about the world of work in a factory today and in Lowry's time and about the problems of working in the countryside.

All this work was particularly supported by drama to reinforce the children's empathy for the content of their work and also encompassed a wide range of other subjects. Their observations were recorded in a variety of visual media including poetry, videos and photographs. This material was shared with other year groups to engender a sense of purpose and to challenge the children with the need to communicate the substance of their research and findings with others.

CASE STUDY 4
'CARRIE'S WAR' BY NINA BAWDEN
AGE: 8/9 YEARS
TIME: ONE WHOLE TERM
FICTION BASED

A work of fiction is used as the basis for work throughout the school and every Spring term different age groups chose different books. The choice of 'Carrie's War' was very good because it could be related to the history of Plymouth during the 1939/45 war. Plymouth was very heavily blitzed – there are still shells of buildings left standing and preserved as a record of the war – and a very rich vein of resource material is available at the Records Office, and through the photographs held in the archives of the local newspaper.

The children collected and brought to school artefacts of the period and set up a war museum. The Royal Marine Band gave a concert in the school hall to provide an excellent background to a 1940s day. For this event the children made food to war-time recipes (which everyone thought tasted awful!) and everyone, including visiting parents, dressed up in 1940s clothes. A grandmother who used to sing with ENSA shared her repertoire of war-time songs with the visitors.

Part way through the project, we evacuated an agreed group of children in role to North Devon. They left the school labelled and carrying their gas masks for a residential experience as evacuees. Their feelings about this evacuation were shared with other children when they returned at the end of the week.

Through these re-enactments of the war the children were able to understand the meaning and significance of this work of fiction and they were able to respond with standards of work that simple studies of the text would be unlikely to promote.

PLANNING THEMATIC WORK

This kind of thematic work depends on really effective group planning. All teachers involved need to know their role, how their strengths can be used to advantage and what exactly the children are going to learn at each stage of the project. Planning takes place in three stages. Stages 1 and 2 are undertaken about three weeks before the end of term in preparation for the work of the following term.

STAGE 1.

The teachers of each year group decide upon a theme for the following term in relation to the appropriate curriculum spiral. They then brainstorm every conceivable idea that might be included in the chosen theme.

STAGE 2.

The group then refine this brainstorming towards more realistic ends by asking themselves the following questions:

○ What do we want to include in this theme?

○ How will it fit into the available time?

○ What is essential to include in this theme?

○ What else do we want to include?

STAGE 3.

This takes place every week throughout the term at after school planning session in two hours of directed time.

This is the detailed weekly planning that ensures work is matched to the needs of different children and that teacher strengths are used to advantage.

Part of the time is spent analysing the previous weeks planning and making decisions about how it could best be further developed. By using a high-lighting system, the planning documentation becomes a record of what was actually taught to each group of children.

Other planning also takes place for those areas of the curriculum not encompassed by the theme.

(Examples of these three stages of planning are included in the detailed documentation of teaching projects in Part 2 of this publication).

2.3. THE SPIRAL CURRICULUM

At Thornbury, because a thematic approach is used and the staff want to ensure that the issues of continuity and progression are addressed, the curriculum is divided into three distinct spirals[1]. The word spiral implies that teachers are always trying to build upon children's previous achievements and experiences.

There is one spiral for each term and they may provide a focus to develop work that has depth and breadth. Most areas of the curriculum fit naturally into a thematic approach but there are some, as are previously described, that are best taught separately to ensure a sequential development related to the children's needs.

SPIRAL 1. AUTUMN TERM
A CONCENTRIC GROUP OF THEMES

This spiral is particularly designed to start from where the child is in his or her understanding at the age of five. It is planned to move in a wider circle each year, building upon previous knowledge and moving from the child and the family, to the school, to the community of Thornbury and then into the wider community of the City and the world outside.

The nature of this spiral imposes a subject focus and this becomes the starting point from which curriculum balance across the year is achieved.

SPIRAL 2. SPRING TERM
FICTION BASED THEMES

This model is planned around fiction based work. It is the term in which we focus upon language and on personal, social and moral education. The works of fiction are chosen carefully to reflect both the needs of the children and the needs of the curriculum, It is important that all the teachers working with the same book are in sympathy with it and feel comfortable working within its concepts. The key factor in any fiction based work is to develop positive links between events within the story and the children's own concepts. For example, unless the children have a concept of poverty – the making of cabbage soup in association with the study of 'Charlie and the Chocolate Factory' becomes a somewhat tenuous activity! The description in the previous section of those activities used to reinforce children's understanding of 'Carrie's War' are typical of ways in which to make the book a real event and not just something to be 'illustrated'.

SPIRAL 3. SUMMER TERM
A WIDE VARIETY OF THEMES·

This is the most flexible of the three spirals. This term is used to balance aspects of the curriculum that have not been covered in the Autumn and Spring terms. Unlike the other spirals which are basically one term, one theme, this spiral could follow that pattern or encompass two or more themes.

If it happens that for a particular year group, Spiral 1 has a historical focus and Spiral 2 an environmental focus then Spiral 3 would have to be biased towards science and technology to create the right balance across the year.

The summer term spiral is determined both by the need to have a balance of subject teaching across the year and to ensure that the schools guidelines in each of the subject disciplines are satisfied for that year group. The subject guidelines lay down in detail those concepts and skills that the majority of each year group is expected to achieve in that particular year.

The National Curriculum programmes of study and attainment targets fit comfortably into this pattern of teaching and a cross-curricular approach can in fact make the task easier but it does need very careful planning.

2.4. MAKING THE ART AND DESIGN CURRICULUM WORK

It is very important to have a clear organisational structure which will support and develop work in all areas of the primary school curriculum. The teachers in this school are supported in their work in art and design through the use of the following structure.

ART AND DESIGN POLICY

The curriculum leader for art and design, through discussion and negotiation with her colleagues, has prepared a detailed art and design policy statement. This provides a framework for those principles that support the work in art and design throughout the school and gives detailed guidance as to the structure and sequence of its teaching. This structure is discussed in some detail in Chapter 4.

IN-SERVICE SUPPORT

Teachers in this school receive in-service support at different levels depending upon their needs. They have opportunities to work alongside each other to learn new skills and different methods of approach. The curriculum leader will set up occasional school based sessions in art and design in order that the whole staff can share in and discuss together aspects of the art and design curriculum. Teachers are encouraged to attend in-service courses at local, county and national level in order to relate their work in this school to a wider perspective.

ORGANISATION AND MATERIALS

There is a highly structured school policy for the use, storage and distribution of materials, equipment and resources. This ensures that teachers and children alike know exactly what is available, where to find it and how to use it! All art areas are set up in the same way across the school; they are colour coded red, clearly labelled and all contain the same basic materials, the idea being that not only an eleven-year-old, but a five-year-old would recognise an 'art area' and have access to quality materials.

FINANCE

Care is taken to match the needs of the subject with proper financial support from year to year, to ensure that standards are maintained and developments accounted for. It is accepted that good quality work can only be generated through the use of good quality materials and equipment.

USE OF DISPLAY

There is a clear policy on the necessary standards for the display and presentation of children's work. Many

Fig. 2.1. Group Planning. The teachers working with Year 5 discussing the next project and its implementation.

valuable teaching points can be made to staff, parents and children by the way in which work is displayed. Wherever possible the work is displayed together with the resources that generated it and in such sequence as to help the onlooker see how it has developed. Another important aspect of promoting display is the development of (a) children providing their own displays of quality, and (b) teachers setting up interactive displays that require thought about the labels and the questions asked.

TIME

Time is used to good purpose by ensuring that sufficient time is set aside for the work in hand and to enable the children to have the opportunity to pursue their work in some depth. As the children move through the school, time for art and design is used more flexibly and by years 5 and 6 the children are likely to have more concentrated time for their work in art and design but at longer intervals.

RESOURCES

As will be evident through the descriptions of work in the accompanying Case Studies and in the detailed description of Themes in Part 2, the staff make a rich use of a wide range of resource material of all kinds in support of their work with the children. A detailed list of all the resources used in the year's work at the school is included as Appendix One (pages 117 to 127).

[1]The spiral curriculum is one where essentially the same fundamental content is encountered throughout but the way it is encountered and the meanings and values it will have are dependant upon the particular stage the learner is at.

Allison, B. (1978), 'Sequential Learning in Art', Journal of the National Society for Art Education, October 1978. pp 6- 14.

Fig. 2.2. Didactic use of display to show development of work on 'Plymouth as a City' project.

ART AND DESIGN IN THE GENERAL EDUCATION OF CHILDREN

3.1. ITS PLACE AND PURPOSE

Art, craft and design are essential components in the curriculum of Thornbury Primary School. The experience of learning how to draw and paint and how to design and make images and artefacts is valuable to children in its own right. Through these means, the children acquire useful communication and making skills. Additionally, their work in the visual arts makes a significant contribution to the quality of the children's learning in many other areas of the school's curriculum.

> *Literacy and numeracy are seen as traditional key elements of the curriculum, each having a unique part to play in the development of the child. However, we believe that it is through 'The Arts' that the child can effectively explore and propose different realities. The arts for us are not self-generating but central to our curriculum, providing a natural form for expression and communication.*

(Thornbury Primary School, Art and Design Policy Statement)

In the early years of schooling, children's work in drawing and painting both supports and extends their development of language. It becomes the focus for much of their naming and knowing about the world. The simple language of symbols that they use in their early drawings enables them to 'tell stories' and to describe their experiences much more freely and flexibly than they can through the more formal means of writing. Through drawing and painting young children are able to make significant statements about their experience in the world and this encourages and enriches their use of language.

In working with materials, in learning how to shape and form in two and three dimensions, children acquire and develop making and handling skills that will form the basis for craftsmanship and technical accomplishment.

Learning to draw with some competence provides children with the essential means to investigate and respond to evidence that is a crucial support to much of their work in the humanities, environmental studies, science and technology.

Children are taught to draw with competence in order to acquire essential skills which will support their work across the curriculum. They should be able to:

○ describe and record the appearance of the natural and made world accurately and sensitively;

○ compare and analyse the structure and appearance of familiar things within the environment;

○ convey factual information through a series of images;

○ tell stories visually;

○ communicate and express ideas that are personal and individual to them.

The children's involvement in the making of images and artefacts plays an important part in the development of their abilities to appraise and reflect upon the appearance and design of many of those things that are an important part of their social and cultural environment. Through the rich use of evidence of the work of artists/designers and craft workers in association with their own work, the children come to a better understanding of the relationship between their own work in school and that in the world outside the school.

At Thornbury, in the making of art – in framing ideas visually – the children are given essential opportunities to explore and communicate their response to both the real world of their surroundings and of the world within themselves. The making of art therefore has an important part to play in their emotional development, in addition to providing them with valuable intellectual, visual and technical skills.

3.2. ART AND DESIGN IN THE GENERAL EDUCATION OF CHILDREN

The value of art and design as a vehicle for promoting learning in the overall development of children's education cannot be emphasised enough. It is vitally important that children are helped to realise that art and design are a part of their everyday life. A visually

Fig 3.1. Reception class children making observed drawing of star fish (chalks and pastels)

Fig 3.2. Observed drawing of a telephone. Year 1. (paint and pastel)

Fig 3.3. Drawing of houses at Dartmouth. Year 5. (chalk on dark ground)

Fig 3.4. Drawing of "my favourite part of the story from Rasco and the Rats of Nihm". Year 5. (biro)

aware teacher can heighten this awareness by involving children in quality experiences which are real and which add relevance, depth and breadth to their present area of study and level of ability.

One of the most challenging roles for the teacher is the task of improving a child's aesthetic awareness: how can children be made aware of the quality and nature of the natural and made world and given the desire to respond to it in many different ways? By seizing every opportunity and taking time at the right moment for description and discussion using rich vocabulary. By valuing the children and their perceptions of the world and things around them. By providing the right stimulus when natural opportunities are non-existent.

Children need to be given opportunities to look, to talk, to make comparisons and to draw conclusions. The experience needs to start from where the child is and be exciting enough to promote a 'rage to learn'.

Most teachers are exceptionally good at talking — both to children and with them. The single most important element of any curriculum is the development of children's oral language through stimulating interactive discussion which immediately involves them in the development of their senses. This in turn promotes their visual vocabulary.

In art and design, talking and drawing go hand in hand. Both the talking and the drawing can provide strategies for helping children to observe closely and this is an essential support to other areas of the curriculum. They can open discussion about line, pattern, texture, colour, tone and form and this in turn heightens the children's awareness of the world around them. Their curiosity is stimulated through questioning how, why, who or when.

A well-organised art and design curriculum delivered by an enthusiastic teacher helps children to make sense of their own experiences. It is an exciting starting point for all areas of the curriculum because most children enjoy talking, doing and interacting. Art and design is most important because, while only one component of the curriculum, through this discipline many forms of learning and expression take place. When looking at any one subject it is essential to identify the skills and concepts that need to be taught. It is important to look at where they overlap other curriculum areas thus allowing the teacher to reinforce elements when needs be and to avoid unnecessary repetition.

Across the whole curriculum, observation in the widest sense of the word, emerges as an essential skill to be learnt by all children. Art and design are obviously the very best vehicles for advancing this aspect of children's work. Through working with art and design children learn to record, analyze, communicate and express themselves. They develop a whole range of expertise in areas that could be referred to as life skills. These are skills which as adults we find invaluable. The children engaged in this type of work have:

○ a better oral and visual vocabulary;

○ more awareness of the world around them;

○ more ability to organise their thinking;

○ more understanding of other cultures and religions;

○ more ability to make reasoned judgments;

○ more ability to solve problems and face challenges;

○ more skills to test their hypotheses;

○ the ability to deal with more than one variable;

○ more ability to make choices about methods of working;

○ experience in working both co-operatively and independently.

As a result they become more creative, inventive and expressive.

Turning to look at the curriculum in broad terms such as the arts, humanities, science and technology, maths, physical education and language development it is immediately obvious that all the above skills play some part in each area.

Art and language are both important means of communication and expression. Oral language goes hand in hand with image making — how often do we listen to a child with a poor vocabulary drawing a really detailed and expressive picture to make a point or share an experience? For some children, drawing is easier, quicker or even more exciting than writing. Every teacher believes children should write. Do they also feel that oral language and drawing are equally important?

It is through the arts that a child can effectively explore and propose different realities. They are a natural form for expression and communication while at the same time retaining their own intrinsic qualities. It is important to understand their relationship with each other and the rest of the curriculum. For example within an identified theme a piece of drama associated with history could, through real empathy, lead to excellent work in art, improvised music, writing or all three of these outcomes. It is very important to promote depth in this type of work rather than tenuous links.

Art and design and humanities share a number of similar concepts. They have roots in other cultures and communities and draw conclusions about how people used to live and what influenced them. When looking at some of the real humanities concepts such as cause and effect, similarity and difference, continuity and change, communication, values and beliefs and stewardship it is easy to see some very strong links between the two areas of study. Teachers need to think carefully about the types of stimuli needed to enhance a child's thought processes — a real and relevant experience could encompass everything from an outside visit or visitor, to the use of three-dimensional artefacts or examples of the visual arts. A critical studies approach [1] not only gives children the opportunity to look at how a particular artist worked but it also allows the child to study the social and

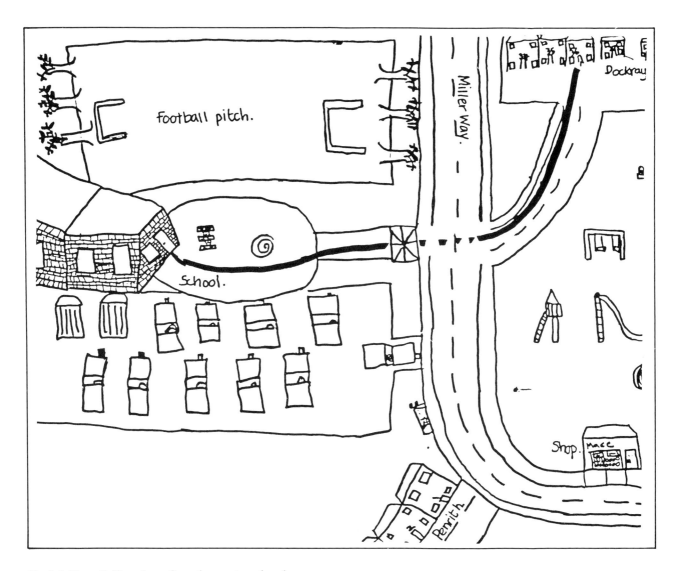

Fig 3.5. Year 2. How I get from home to school.
Annotated drawing (fibre pen)

Fig 3.6. Year 2. The weight lifter. Annotated drawing.
(fibre tip)

cultural setting of that time.

Many children draw, paint, re-create and talk about artefacts which are concerned with industrial archaeology. Is this art and design or is it environmental studies? Science too has its foundations in close looking, analyzing, testing hypotheses and communicating. When children are involved in seeking patterns, looking at space and shape, one could ask the question is this maths, or science, or art?

Obviously many areas of study overlap and the intelligent teacher will use this to best advantage to reinforce children's previous knowledge and encourage them to make links that help make sense of the world around them. No child should be put in the position of learning in compartments: a well-structured art and design policy helps enrich and extend children's learning across the curriculum.

The best learning experiences take place in schools where adults and children trust each other, where both are relaxed and happy. Everyone needs to feel valued for what they have to offer, this in turn allows experimentation to take place without fear of failure. It provides for excitement and continual development – in other words, the living, changing, growing school.

3.3. THE DEVELOPMENT OF CHILDREN'S IMAGE MAKING

Drawing and painting have a very special function for young children. They provide them with a form of communication that is both more flexible and precise than the formal language of the written or spoken word.

Young children come to terms with a strange and exciting world by 'naming' it visually. The images they produce are absolutely related to their ideas about and their knowledge of the world. Their drawings stand for or 'symbolise' their view of the world. They do not represent it. The images they make and their meaning may change several times in the process of making.

When the child's vocabulary is limited to a few hundred words, the making of a drawing enables him or her to make more complex statements than words will allow. Making an image supports children in their thinking in addition to helping them to name and describe their world and to respond to and enjoy its complexities.

Until the age of six or seven, children are not able to analyze their response to the environment. They tend to select that aspect of a thing or person that will best identify it for them – hence the domination of images of the head in children's early drawings of people. Their drawing has little reference to formal or traditional forms of visual expression – nor are they confused by the differences between the images they make and the appearance of the real world. They happily kaleidoscope time, space and scale in one

drawing and it is this very quality that gives the work of young children that vitality of expression that often begins to wane as they develop the ability to handle the formal tools of communication. As soon as they are able to convey their thoughts, ideas and feelings through the written and spoken word, the emotive drive to communicate through visual means begins to wind down simply because it can be satisfied in other ways. At the same time, children begin to develop the ability to see and respond to the world independently of their feelings. They become more objective, more aware of existing visual forms and images and the apparent authority of those forms: more aware of the complexity of the visual environment and the problem of interpreting the 'real' world. They become more conscious of the differences between the images they make and those that surround them.

The point at which children recognise that the images they make have public consequence is a crucial one, because it is here that they begin to compare and relate their drawings of all those images of the real world that surround them in photographs and in film and television.

At Thornbury School, the teachers support the children's desire to make 'real' images in very positive ways. They provide source materials and other resources to help develop the looking and focusing that encourage children to investigate and communicate through their image and model-making, as well as promoting personal and imaginative responses.

Much of this is achieved simply through recognising that this transition takes place. It is important to understand that children move from drawing symbolically towards drawing descriptively and transactionally, and that it is necessary to provide opportunities for them to use both systems of drawing from the beginning of their schooling. As soon as children have acquired the basic skills of making those simple shapes that may be used in various combinations to both stand for and represent the things they want to record, they are happily 'bilingual' in their use of imagery.

At Thornbury, children are encouraged to use drawing in a variety of ways. In the Reception and Infants classes they use a developing vocabulary of shape and colour to make both 'story telling' and 'careful looking' drawings and paintings. The children draw symbolically and quite naturally as an extension to their work in language and to explain to each other and to their teacher their understanding of their latest experiences. Alongside this they are gradually introduced to the conventions of drawing descriptively and where it is appropriate to the content of their work, they are encouraged to work from observation of simple and everyday things. These 'careful looking' drawings are generated through that kind of discussion and questioning that helps young children to focus upon and seek out and record those simple qualities that describe familiar things.

As their confidence grows in the making and management of images the children are encouraged to use

Fig 3.7. Using talk as a focus for looking. Teacher and child from Year 5 sharing a view of the environment at the Beaford Residential Centre

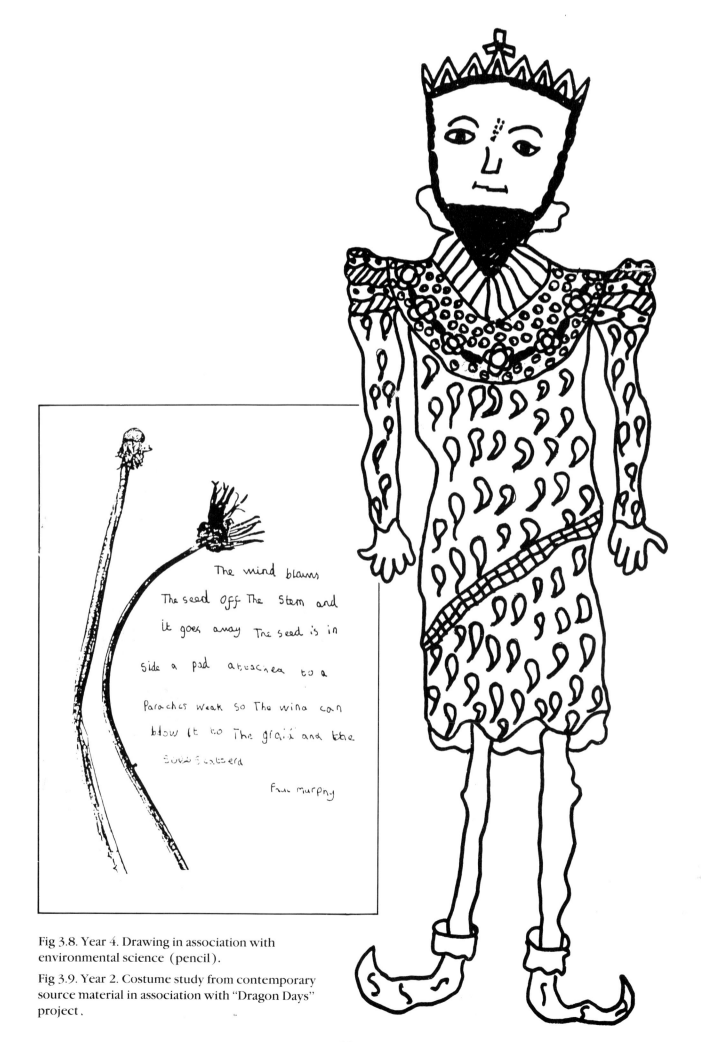

The mind blows
The seed off The stem and
it goes away The seed is in
side a pad attached to a
Parachus weak so The wind can
blow it to The grass and the
seed scatterd

Paul Murphy

Fig 3.8. Year 4. Drawing in association with
environmental science (pencil).

Fig 3.9. Year 2. Costume study from contemporary
source material in association with "Dragon Days"
project.

drawing and painting more transactionally, as a means of investigation and analysis and for the exploration of ideas. The methodologies that support this development are described in more detail in Chapter 5 'Drawing and Painting'.

It is characteristic of the school that the development of image making, related to the children's changing perceptions of themselves and their environment, is taken as seriously as the management of language and the development of mathematical concepts. The children are set tasks that are appropriate to their stage of perception. The work they do in art and design always has a specific purpose and is properly related to their needs.

Because their work in art and design has this sense of purpose and is properly supportive of their learning across the curriculum, the children use drawing and painting, and designing and making, naturally and unselfconsciously. It is an activity that has real sense and meaning for them.

3.4. MAKING AND APPRAISING

Appraisal and reflection follow naturally upon the making of images and artefacts. At Thornbury, the teachers are encouraged to use appraisal as a positive support to the children's work and in order to ensure that they give it value.

Initially, appraisal grows out of that rich use of language which supports all the work in the school. Children are encouraged to talk about their work to the teacher and to each other in describing what they have done: they begin to value what has been learnt and understood and achieved.

Questioning and discussion are often used very directly so that children are required to consider a particular stage of their work and how it might be further developed. For example:

○ Is that the right shade of pink?

○ How are you going to change that colour?

○ Can you see both ears?

○ What shaped piece of paper do you need to start with?

As the children move through the school, progressively greater use is made of the work of other artists, craftspeople and designers to help them begin to see the connections between their own work and that of others and to place their own work in context. 'Knowing about' art and design is seen to be as important as being able to make it. Looking at the work of others is valued for what may be learnt through considering the various ways that other artists and designers have worked upon similar tasks and themes to those presented to the children.

The children learn about colour by making colour, by observing colours in the real world and by looking at how different painters use colour and make colour and apply colour in different ways. Initially the work

is often mimetic and the children 'borrow' from the work of others. As they grow in their understanding of their own work, the work of other artists is used to focus a task or theme to help them to see the expressive possibilities within the context of the theme. This year, for example, children studied Rousseau's paintings in association with a visit to the tropical house at Paignton Zoo; Klee's cityscapes were used to help the children see how they might extend their own studies of the city centre in Plymouth; and reference was made to the work of the Newlyn school of painters to support a day visit to a Cornish harbour.

Evidence of the work of artists and designers is also richly used to provide contemporary evidence of times past or of different places or cultures – especially in association with humanities projects.

In these various ways a positive link is established between making and appraisal and between action and reflection. The children are helped to a better understanding of their own work through this combination of reflection and appraisal and use of the work of others. More importantly, they also have access to a wider range of possibilities in their use of visual language than children in schools where the only art they see is their own.

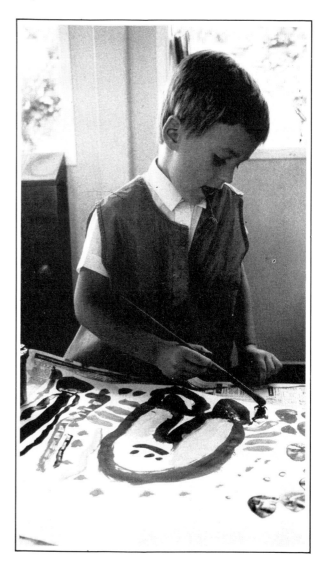

Fig 3.10. Child in Reception class engaged in making an early "symbolic" painting.

Figs 3.11. a) and b). Children's ability to draw bi-lingually in the early years of their schooling. A contrast between a "story telling" drawing from Year 1 and children in the Reception class making "careful looking" drawings.

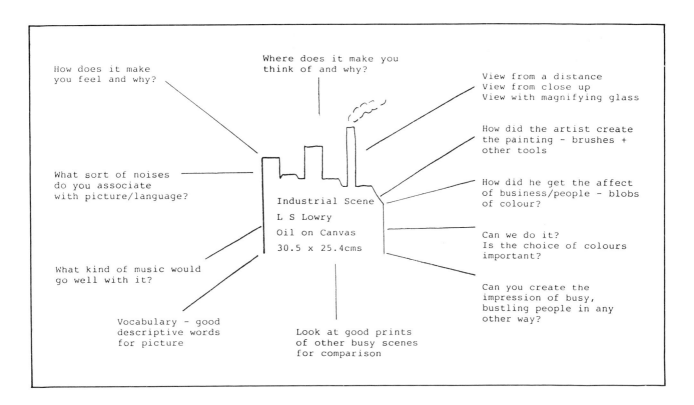

How does it make
you feel and why?

Where does it make you
think of and why?

View from a distance
View from close up
View with magnifying glass

How did the artist create
the painting - brushes +
other tools

What sort of noises
do you associate
with picture/language?

Industrial Scene
L S Lowry
Oil on Canvas
30.5 x 25.4cms

How did he get the affect
of business/people - blobs
of colour?

Can we do it?
Is the choice of colours
important?

What kind of music would
go well with it?

Can you create the
impression of busy,
bustling people in any
other way?

Vocabulary - good
descriptive words
for picture

Look at good prints
of other busy scenes
for comparison

Fig 3.12. Looking at and using the work of other artists. Diagram from Thornbury Art and Design policy to illustrate the various ways that artist's work may be approached.

Fig 3.13. Year 3. 'Mimetic' drawing from an industrial landscape by L S Lowry

Fig 3.14. Year 5. Drawing of a cornish harbour
(pencil and biro) made from observation and after
referring to the work of painters from the Newlyn
School.

STRUCTURE AND SEQUENCE IN ART AND DESIGN

4.1. PLACING THE WORK IN CONTEXT FOR CHILDREN

The description, in Chapter 2, of the way that the curriculum is organised at Thornbury Primary School, outlines how the children's learning is placed within a real context for them. The children's world of learning begins within their investigation of themselves and their immediate concerns and spirals out into the more complex exploration of their community, their city and the world beyond.

In all this work there is an over-riding concern to make the children's learning real to them and to set them tasks and challenges that are rooted within their own experience. This principle, that children learn most effectively where the curriculum touches them most closely and personally is at the heart of the school's thinking. History has more meaning for children where it begins with the history of their own family through the study of its memorabilia, or through seeking evidence of the past within their own community.

Similarly, their work in art and design has more meaning for them when it begins with the visual exploration of their immediate world, their possessions and familiar things within the environment: or when it is used to enable them to recall events important to them or to re-tell and embroider upon favourite stories.

There is constant reference in Chapters 2 and 3 to the ways in which oral language is used to generate learning and, in Chapter 5 which concentrates on the teaching of drawing, there is a similar focus upon the importance of talk and discussion to support children's perception of their world.

This marriage of language to experience, which epitomises the best of the teaching at Thornbury, is the most significant factor in the design of the school's curriculum. In the teaching of art and design there is a similar marriage between providing the children with a rich variety of visual experience and engaging their perception of that experience through talk and discussion.

Through this means, the children's work in art and design is placed in context for them. Their making of images and artefacts becomes a natural way of responding to their experience of the world. It has a sense of purpose for them and helps them to place their work in art and design centrally within their learning.

4.2. SEQUENCE AND STRUCTURE WITHIN PROJECTS

The school's Art and Design Policy establishes a clear framework for the planning of work in art and design related to the various themes that are encompassed within the school's curriculum.

This planning takes place within the overall structure for the development of year themes as described in the previous chapter. The art and design planning sheets are set out in such a way as to encourage teachers to consider how they might develop a range of art and design activities related to the class theme and how these activities might stem from initial investigation into a variety of activities.

The work is planned under the following headings:
EXPERIENCE/STIMULUS MEDIA – visits, resources, arts experiences etc.

KEY SKILL TEACHING POINTS – design, line, colour, pattern, texture, shape, form.

EXTENSION OF ACTIVITY – painting, textiles, ceramics, print, modelling, collage.

IMAGINATIVE ELEMENTS – subjective activity.

The example below shows how one teacher has planned a module of work in ceramics for children in Year 2 as part of their fiction based project 'James and the Giant Peach' (this project is described in detail in Part 2, pages 88 – 94).

These planning sheets do require teachers to think carefully about the range of resources they will use to establish a rich experience for the children and which will initiate purposeful enquiry within the theme. The time spent on this initial investigation is time well invested. A combination of observation, talk, inter-action, discussion and reflection allows the children time to grasp the purpose of the task. When matched to different combinations of experience this initial investigation extends the children's understanding of possibilities within the task.

Figure 4.2. illustrates how one teacher uses reproductions of paintings and sculptures and discussion about these, in combination with the children working in groups to observe each other huddled and sleeping under blankets. This is the preliminary investigation to making drawings and then clay models of people sheltering during the air-raids in the 1939/45 war and was part of the 'Plymouth Past' theme described in detail in Part 2 (pages 79 – 85).

The range and balance of resources used throughout the school is impressive and these are detailed in the Appendix (pages 125 – 135) they include natural and manufactured forms, photographs, visits, events, works of art and literature. Over the years, the school has built up its own significant bank of resources to generate enquiry and to support the range of themes used across the curriculum. An intensive use is also made of resources within the local community – people, places, artefacts and events, and from such sources as the County's Learning Resources Service.

The following list of the resources used in the Year 2 project on 'Ourselves' gives some indications of how much value is placed upon using resources to both generate and focus enquiry.

NATURAL THINGS

Hands
Eyes
Ears
Face
Fingerprints
Tropical fruits
Vegetables
Plants
Fleece
Textured objects

PHOTOGRAPHS AND PHOTO COPIES

Old faces
Young faces
Cats eyes
Owls eyes
Gloves
Hands

MANUFACTURED THINGS

Meals
Menus
Plates
Telephones
Teddy bears
Musical instruments
Crisp and sweet wrappers
Bottles
Concave and convex lenses
Mirrors

VISITS

Conservation area
Plymbridge Woods
Events
Touch trail
Parent to talk about child's blindness

WORKS OF ART

Van Gogh
Picasso
Escher

The use of resources in this way naturally supports that investigation through drawing which is central to all the work in art and design at Thornbury. The structure for the teaching of drawing and its extension into painting is described in detail in the following chapter. Considerable attention is given to the different ways in which drawing can be used to initiate those different kinds of enquiry that are needed to support themes as contrasting as those that are fiction based or industry based.

The school's Art and Design Policy provides a detailed structure for the teaching of each of the art and design disciplines. The way in which art and design projects are planned within the themes encourages the teachers to seek connections across these different disciplines and to use enquiry through drawing as the base for other work in painting or in any of the craft and design fields

Figure 4.3. describes how a local study through drawing of the variety of front and back doors to be found in the neighbourhood may be extended into a design activity and then into work in relief in clay and other materials.

4.3 OVERALL BALANCE OF THE WORK IN ART AND DESIGN

In Chapter 3.1, in describing the place and purpose of work in art and design within the Thornbury curriculum, there is reference to the way in which balance is sought in the teaching of drawing to ensure that the children acquire a variety of drawing skills. These are needed to ensure that drawing is used purposefully to match those different kinds of investigation and enquiry that children have to undertake in different aspects of the curriculum.

These different ways of using drawing are explored in more detail in the following chapter.

In addition to seeking a balance of different kinds of art and design activities for the children as they move through the school, there is concern to seek a balance of those different purposes for which art and design may be used. These are detailed in the Art and Design Policy as follows:

DESCRIBING – close observation, real stimulus, natural/manmade objects, critical studies

ANALYSIS – selecting a large/small area of interest, use of focusing devices

COMMUNICATION – visual story telling, diagrams and annotated drawings to convey information and facts

PROBLEM-SOLVING – working drawings, planning, colour diaries, choice of media

EXPRESSION – imaginative and personal expression

The Art and Design Policy also contains the charts illustrated in Figure 4.4. which identify for teachers how these different categories of working in art and design may be identified within typical programmes for Year 3 (fiction based project 'Charlotte's Web') and Year 6.

Although there is obviously some considerable overlap between these different ways of working in art and design, this planning device does help teachers to keep a proper balance of purpose in mind and

Fig 4.1. Planning Sheet. Year 2. "James and Giant Peach"

Spring 1989

DESIGN AND ART PLANNING Group Name: *Middle Infant Ceramics* Week Ending: *1st cycle – 10/2*

EXPERIENCE/ STIMULUS	MEDIA	KEY SKILL TEACHING POINTS	EXTENSION OF ACTIVITY	IMAGINATIVE ELEMENTS
visit, resource, arts exp., etc	identify medium	design, line, colour, pattern, texture, shape, form	textiles, ceramics, print, modelling, collage, painting	subjective activity
'James & the Giant Peach' descriptions of James, Aunt Spiker & Aunt Sponge. *Discussion.*	*Clay.*	*Construction of 'coil' character, developed to convey the characteristics of chosen subject. Development of skills: rolling 'sausages' of clay of different length & thickness and joining with slip to create basic form which can be developed with additional modelling, pinching etc, texture and pattern … created with modelling tools & objects. Use of slips, underglaze colour & c/w glaze. Develop awareness of fining processes & appropriate language.*	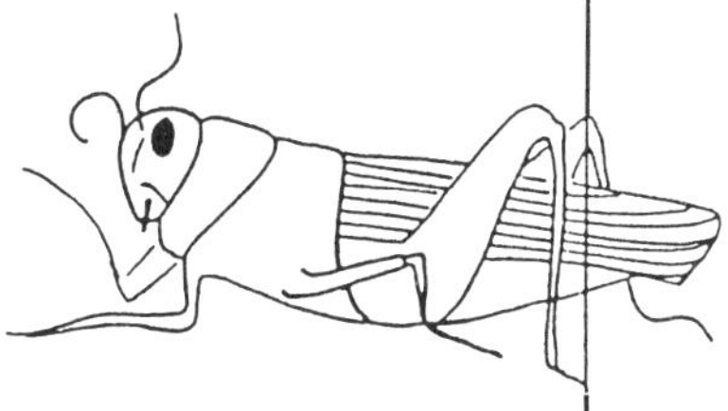	*Personal interpretation*
Passages from book. *Ideas evoked through ongoing work & discussion*		*Wks 3 & 4 Creation of 'group piece' – 3D peach. Hollow form created by lining large spherical 'mould'. Group modelling of interior walls & furniture etc.*		
Close up photographs of insects to focus on joints etc. Minibeast specimens. Passages from 'James & the Giant Peach'.		*Focus on shape and structure of individual insects… eg how many legs? Where are their joints? Wings? What features make each an individual? Shape, pattern, texture. Characteristics of insects from book – eg. centipede's boots etc.*		*personal interpretations of characters*
	Clay	*Portraits of 'insects' Development of skills – rolling coils, pellets of various size, length & thickness… joining elements to create basic form of chosen subject… develop with additional modelling, texture, pattern. Use of slip, underglaze colour, glaze etc.*	*Create convex form to represent surface of peach, onto which insects could be joined – gp/ind?*	

Fig 4.2. Planning Sheet. Year 5. "Plymouth Past"

Summer 1989

DESIGN AND ART PLANNING Group Name: *Year 5* Week Ending: *1st 3 week cycle – 29/9*

EXPERIENCE/ STIMULUS	MEDIA	KEY SKILL TEACHING POINTS	EXTENSION OF ACTIVITY	IMAGINATIVE ELEMENTS
visit, resource, arts exp., etc	identify medium	design, line, colour, pattern, texture, shape, form	textiles, ceramics, print, modelling, collage, painting	subjective activity
Henry Moore's 'Four grey sleepers' and other shelter drawings (slides) 2D reproductions of the following sculptures: Giacometti 'Reclining Woman', Moore 'Reclining Mother & Child', 'Reclining Figure' etc. Wotruba 'Reclining figure'		*Discuss the use of line to show 3D form of figures. Consider the position of the sleeping/reclining body – shapes created by the position of limbs; how do drapes (bankets etc) emphasize contours of body? Look at proportion (distorted for emphasis in many sculptures) – observe children in group adopting 'favourite sleeping position'*		
	Microliner Compressed charcoal	*(i) use line only to describe form, (ii) use shading to create 3D drawing*		
Children in the group *Cushions & blankets*	*clay*	*Creating 3D model of reclining/sleeping figure based on obs. studies. Skills to develop:- Use of pinched and modelled coils to create basic figure shape; rolling very fine slabs of clay to drape; use of modelling tools & fingers for mod. detail; use of slip. Solving problems of support as necessary. Fining & oxiding figures.*		

Fig 4.3. Planning Sheet. Year 3. "Houses & Homes"

Autumn 1989

DESIGN AND ART PLANNING   Group Name: *(1st Year) – Year 3*   Week Ending: *1st cycle Thurs 11-11.50am until half term*

EXPERIENCE/ STIMULUS	MEDIA	KEY SKILL TEACHING POINTS	EXTENSION OF ACTIVITY	IMAGINATIVE ELEMENTS
visit, resource, arts exp., etc	identify medium	design, line, colour, pattern, texture, shape, form	textiles, ceramics, print, modelling, collage, painting	subjective activity
Front & back doors of childrens' homes. *Slides & photographs/ copies: (i) of a wide variety of doors eg, in houses of different periods and styles; castles; stately homes etc …; (ii) of decorative features; door knockers, handles, numbers, letter boxes etc.; (iii) of a range of homes with the doors deleted.* *Working designs for doors*	*pencils – range* *clay*	*1. Focus on (i) whole door and its frame, doorstep etc.; (ii) moving closer to look at an area of interest; (iii) closer still to observe detail of a small section.* *3 sketches, prior to first session, to look at shape, line, pattern & texture.* *2. Look at a wide variety of doors and the buildings to which they belong – consider suitability; why is a particular door appropriate to one building but not another? What materials is the door made from? What makes it well proportioned? Are there panels, carvings, decorative door posts, mouldings, steps, fanlight etc? How do the handles, letter boxes, door knockers vary?* *3. To create the designed door and its surround.* *Skills to develop: Rolling with rolling pin and guide lines, cutting with knife after sketching shape (– achieving right angles!); developing door with applied and incised detail, modelling and texture. Use of slip.* *Firing process.* *Use of underglaze colours, oxides and glazes as appropriate to each design*	*from the images of buildings with doors deleted select one and 'design a door' with its surround, appropriate for the chosen building.* *Use line to depict shape and enlarge any decorative features to show details.* *Photocopy for adding colour.* 	

Fig 4.4. Planning Sheet. Year 3. "Charlotte's Web"

1ST YEAR DEVELOPMENTS	DRAWING	ADDING COLOUR	DESIGN	PRINTMAKING	TEXTILES, 3D
DESCRIBING (close observation, real stimulus, natural/ man made objects, cr. studies)	Observation of arachnids using real if possible and or photographs, thumb nail sketches of farm – on site observation of farm implements	Direct critical studies/ mimetic work – Breughel, Constable, Monet etc. Use of thumb nail sketches for painting	Enlarge section of spider		Farm hanging
ANALYSIS (selecting a small/ large area of interest, focusing devices, lenses, keyholes etc)	Linear patterns in a spider's web. Looking at comparative structures – networks in nature. Hedgerow composition, observing works of art	Direct work with colour for hedgerow work. Photocopies hedgerow drawings – addition of watercolour focus on area and keyhole for enlarged work	Focus on web area and abstract for design. Focus on hedgerow area and abstract design line	Use of web work to create print for repeat pattern. Use of hedgerow design for single print.	Use of web design for sewn collage. Use of hedgerow design for sewn collage.
COMMUNICATION (visual storytelling, diagrams, annotated drawing)	Use of chosen sequence of events, interpret as a diagram the facial emotions, rage, happy, sad.		patterns for noises and movements, stop, start, push, pull etc. Fairground action sequence for building a web.	Use of patterns to create print/ repeat pattern	The feelings through woven colours. Applique faces.
PROBLEM SOLVING (work drawings, planning colour diaries, choice of paper/ media)	Working drawing of Ferris wheel, roundabout etc	Use of fairground to paint picture			Use of drawings as basis for working models
EXPRESSION (imaginative and creative multi-media picture)	Charlotte's view of the barn. Wilbur's view of Charlotte.	Characters in the story. Eggs. Sky scenes – clouds, raindrops, snow. Feelings painted.	Egg decoration	Batik on egg shape	Models of the characters. Embroidered eggs, egg cosies. Mobiles – what is black

perhaps helps to ensure that over the year their children use art and design flexibly and resourcefully within their learning.

Within each curriculum project there will be a different balance of art and design activities depending upon the nature of the theme. For example, in fiction based projects descriptive and communication based work is likely to dominate – whereas in projects biased towards Science and Technology it is probable that analytical and problem-solving based work will be the main thrust of the enquiry.

THE BALANCE BETWEEN OBJECTIVE AND EXPRESSIVE WORK

Maintaining the right balance between objective work and expressive work with children is probably the most difficult part of putting together a coherent programme of work in art and design in a primary school. There has already been some discussion in Chapter 3 about the way in which children make the transition from drawing symbolically to drawing descriptively in their first three years of schooling. This is further developed in the next chapter on the teaching of drawing which describes how in this school, children are encouraged to make both story-telling and descriptive drawings from the beginning of their schooling 'to encourage them to begin to investigate and communicate through their image and model making as well as to use them for personal and imaginative response'.

When children are provided with interesting visual reference materials and their observation of these is supported by good talk and discussion they will work confidently in their making of descriptive images and models from Year 2 and onwards. However, their confidence in making images from recall or 'from the imagination' becomes more problematical simply because children are reluctant to put to one side the success they may have achieved already in their descriptive and objective work.

In many schools the 'problem' is dealt with by putting expressive based work to one side and by focusing the children's work specifically within the objective arena. This understandable response by teachers is rooted in some misconceptions of the relationship between objective and expressive based work. Children cannot 'create' or 'invent' or 'express' their personal response to their experience in some kind of imaginative vacuum. The ability to 'imagine' or to re-create or re-order experience rests heavily upon children who have been given few experiences to invent upon!

We may frequently wonder at the ability of artists like Picasso and Klee and Hockney to re-invent a whole new world of images and symbols and perhaps ignore the fact this invention is rooted within many years of detailed observation through drawing of the real world of their own experience.

Similarly, children can only imagine or re-invent their own view of the world upon the basis of some knowledge and understanding of that world through their own observations and drawings. Their understanding of the possibilities of the use of visual language will also be extended where they are given an opportunity to observe and discuss the various ways that other artists have responded to similar challenges to those that they face.

In this year, in this school, there were good examples of the way that the children's imagination has been 'fired' through observation of the work of other artists.

Figure 4.5. illustrates the outline planning for a project with children in Year 5, and is a good example of the way a teacher may support expressive based work with children by giving them a combination of objective experience to reinforce their 'imagining'.

This work was undertaken in association with the fiction based project 'Racso and the Rats of Nihm'. The purpose was to help the children to key into what might be a 'rats eye' view of their environment.

During this year in the work at Thornbury Primary School, there were many similar examples of teachers seeking to generate an expressive response from their children by giving them that kind of experience upon which they could 'imagine' with confidence.

[1] Criticial and related contextual studies in art and design are concerned with those aspects of the subject which enable children to express ideas and insights that reflect a developing awareness of the significance of their own work and that of others, including work from different cultures and different times.

Fig 4.5. Planning Sheet. Year 5. "Racso and the Rats of Nihm"

DESIGN AND ART PLANNING   Group Name: *3rd & 4th Year Role play areas 'The Forest' & related extension for 3rd & 4th Year Art and Ceramics*   Week Ending: *6/1 & 13/1. Extension – 10/2*

EXPERIENCE/ STIMULUS	MEDIA	KEY SKILL TEACHING POINTS	EXTENSION OF ACTIVITY	IMAGINATIVE ELEMENTS
visit, resource, arts exp., etc	identify medium	design, line, colour, pattern, texture, shape, form	textiles, ceramics, print, modelling, collage, painting	subjective activity
Paintings by Henri Rousseau, eg, 'Surprise', 'La Cascade', 'Jungle'. Max Ernst's 'La Joie de Vivre', 'Evening Song'. *Collages by Henri Matisse.* *Collection of slides to project as large scale images, ie, a rats eye view of vegetation.* *Conservation area.* *Collection of large plants with a variety of shaped leaves, fronds, structures, eg, ferns, vines, examples of leaves, mushrooms, berries, nuts, etc.* *Magnifying lenses.*	*Pencils for initial sketches to collect ideas and info.* *Collaborative work in small groups to create large scale designs. Chalk.* *Powder paint.*	*Discuss how Rousseau transformed commonplace plants into surreal, almost dreamlike environments.* *Shapes and forms of vegetation are sharply defined and collectively create strong surface pattern. Use Rousseau's work and other stimuli as a basis from which to develop large scale paintings, developing decorative element by exaggerating patterns and textures which become obvious through magnification. SCALE.* *Colour mixing. Range of greens applied as flat areas of colour, to develop with linear pattern & textural effects. Appropriate use of brushes.* *Combine the pieces as appropriate to create role play area*	*3rd Year extension* *Observational drawings of the 'forest' role play environment from various viewpoints.* *From drawings extract main pattern of shapes using line.* *Transfer onto stretched fabric with hot wax. Develop areas of texture with a range of marks ... dribbling wax, dotting, cracking ...* *Easibrush ... colour mixing. Apply to design. Develop design with stitching, wadding, appliqué, cut-out areas (example piece of work as additional stimulus).*	*Individual and group interpretation of ideas.*
Role play area – 'the forest'. *Related stimuli: paintings by Rousseau, Max Ernst etc, designs by William Morris.* *Photographs of leaves etc. Photocopies. Collection of slides to project as large scale images. 'Made slides' to show silhouetted shapes of leaves ... A selection of plants, leaves, berries, nuts, etc.* *Magnifying lenses*	*Pencil 4B – 4H Microliner Brush & indian ink* *Ceramics*	*Discussion of stimuli to focus on nature as designer: patterns created by the shapes and arrangement of leaves, stems, etc, how they relate to create patterns of space between positive elements.* *Close up on textural qualities and linear pattern of veins etc.* *Relative scale – 'rats eye' images.* *Use line to depict these images, creating textures with a variety of marks. Use ink to block in negative spaces to emphasize design of shapes.* *Develop designs onto individual tiles which can be combined to create a group 'screen'.* *Developing skills: using rolling pin and guidelines to roll out slabs from which to cut tiles – discuss.*		

DRAWING AND PAINTING

5.1. THE CENTRAL PLACE OF DRAWING

The central place of drawing in the Thornbury School curriculum has already been described in Chapter 3. Its value is clearly recognised in the way that children are taught to use drawing flexibly and for a variety of purposes. Drawing is the essential underpinning for all work in art, craft and design and is used purposefully to support that kind of investigation that is so essential to much of the children's work in the humanities, in environmental studies and in science and technology.

The strategies used to develop the children's work in drawing are described below. They provide a detailed account of the ways in which drawing is regarded as a serious activity in this school; an activity that has its own disciplines but which also allows children the means to communicate effectively their ideas, their observations and their feelings in response to a wide range of experience.

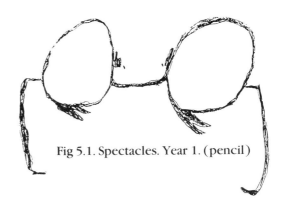

Fig 5.1. Spectacles. Year 1. (pencil)

5.2. DIFFERENT USES FOR DRAWING

The making of images through drawing provides evidence of children's responses to different kinds of experience. It is largely determined by the quality of those experiences and the way that the teacher places them in context. The kind of drawings children make will be influenced by the way that the task

Fig 5.2. Teapots. Year 2
(water colour).

Fig 5.3. Studies of rats. Year 5
(pencil).

is framed for them through the kind of talk and questioning that supports the looking.

The Art and Design Policy at Thornbury provides a framework for the use of drawing by describing its different functions as follows.

DRAWING AS RECORDING

This is the most objective function of drawing where it is used to record and describe the appearance of natural or made objects. Appearance can be recorded for a variety of reasons: for the pleasure to be derived from of looking and knowing as well as recording accurately. It may be used as a means of collecting information about the real world which involves recording, analysing, conjecture and ultimately the communication of information. Whilst the child is involved in recording the appearance of natural and made objects this can be supported by quality oral activity and the provision of quality materials.

DRAWING FOR COMMUNICATION

This kind of drawing helps to convey different information about the world in which we live. It may take the form of a diagram, a pictorial map or visual storytelling. Drawing for communication helps children to use images and symbols and has a vast amount of on-tap source material especially in environmental studies, eg, illustrations of the growth and development of plants or caterpillar/chrysalis/butterfly. Explaining a sequence through pictures provides a good vehicle for learning which involves a variety of techniques. Further examples of communication through images rather than through words can be found in road signs, logos, pop-up books and comic strips.

DRAWING FOR ANALYSIS

This kind of drawing activity takes place when the child is asked to select and isolate elements for particular study. It is important to help the child make sense and order from complex environments, eg,

collections of textures or observation of similarities and differences in the patterns of a shell collection. It is essential that analysis through drawing is clearly related to real objects. All analytical drawing requires careful consideration of the choice of medium children should be encouraged to use, and consideration of the language of the visual elements and principles which can be taught through active looking and talking.

DRAWING AS PROBLEM SOLVING

Problem solving as a function of drawing is particularly significant in the study of how real objects or events function. It involves a high level of oral activity and doing – that is taking apart, reconstruction and invention. Children all need to acquire the related vocabulary, and to develop control of the media as well as the practical aspects of this area. Children should be encouraged to investigate things as they are and learn to represent them from their observations and imagination; they should also be encouraged to communicate how things might be.

DRAWING AS A MEANS OF PERSONAL EXPRESSION

To enable this mode of drawing to take place it is important to consider the context within which drawing takes place. For example, to ask for a drawing of 'How I look' would be vastly different to asking 'How I would like to look'. A good way to encourage expressive drawing is to always consider the vehicle carefully. An excellent ploy is to consider familiar things and change them into strange things, eg, a journey inside their head based on previous discussion about a journey from their home to the house of their friend. The stimulus for personal expression has to be strong and well planned. Evoking images through poetry, dance, music, drama and teacher-built environments can provide an ideal vehicle for personal expression and it can take advantage of the strong stimuli that inter-related arts activities can provide.

We drew the main lines of the design on material using hot wax.....

Communication Drawings. Made to convey information and facts.

Fig 5.4. Year 2. How we made our drawings in batik.

Fig 5.5. Year 3. Playground games

In this school, drawing becomes a real agent in the children's learning because a wide range of drawing methodologies are used. The children are encouraged to use drawing to observe, to invent, to investigate and to analyse the appearance of the real world and to communicate ideas and information.

Fig 5.6. Year 4. The structure of the eye

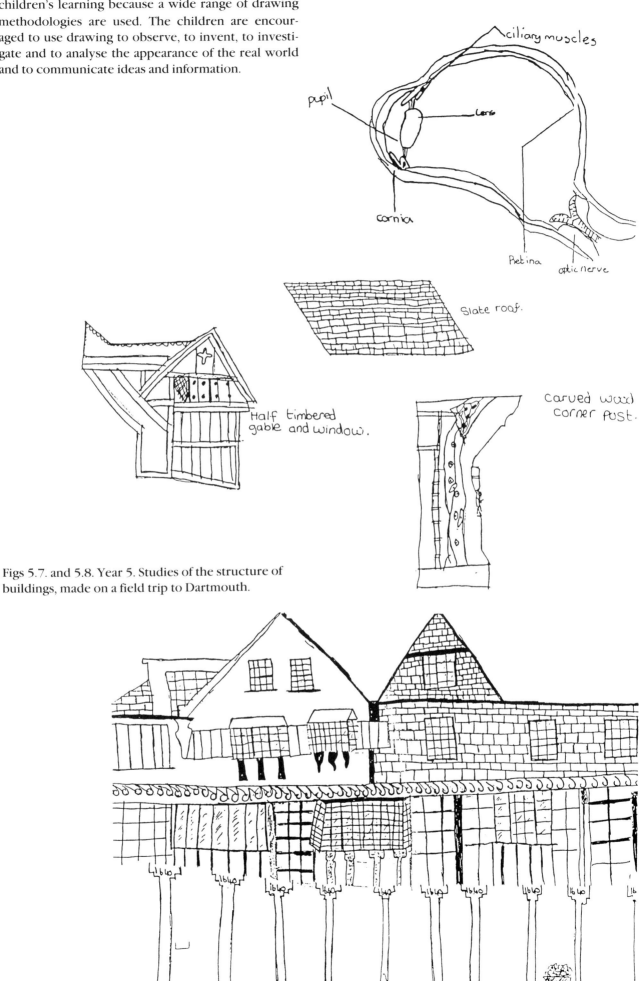

Figs 5.7. and 5.8. Year 5. Studies of the structure of buildings, made on a field trip to Dartmouth.

Figs 5.9. and 5.10. Expressive drawings. Year 5.   'A Rat's Eye View of the World' based upon readings of 'Racso and the Rats of Nihm'.

30

5.3. STRATEGIES FOR TEACHING DRAWING

Reference has already been made in Chapter 2 to the central place that language has in the curriculum of this school:

The single most important element of any curriculum is the development of children's oral language through stimulating interactive discussion which immediately involves them in the development of their senses.

The importance of talk – describing, questioning, discussing – as a support for drawing cannot be over-emphasised. It is through talk as much as through looking that children come to see the world about them more clearly and perceptively. Talk can be used in a variety of ways – the simplest being the way that a series of questions associated with looking can help children to see and select what is before them.

One of the most direct ways to help children to look is to place before them two similar things and ask them to look for the difference between them – simple things like leaves or pebbles or complex things like two children with similar identities, or a pair of semi-detached houses. Comparison makes for careful observation and children become conscious of subtleties of form, colour and surface. Drawing by comparison can become a kind of observation game as when children are asked to draw one of their own fingers so carefully that it is possible to identify straight away which hand it is from and which finger; or sitting several round a table, to draw the eyebrow or nose or mouth of another child so carefully that it can be quickly identified with its owner.

Just as talk can help children to sort out and identify what they are being asked to draw, so can various kinds of focusing devices. The simplest of these serve to isolate what is to be drawn from a complex background. More complex focusing devices, in association with appropriate discussion, can serve to place the drawing within a specific context.

Where children are making studies from complicated forms (eg. small studies of patterns and surfaces taken from a piece of driftwood, an eroded shell etc), it is useful for the children to use a simple viewfinder – a small hole torn in a piece of paper or a rectangle cut in a piece of card, to help them select which bit they are going to draw and to isolate that part for special attention. A familiar focusing device is the magnifying glass or lens; over and above its accepted function of making it easier to see small details clearly, it has the added bonus that, for children, it can place familiar things into a new, and unfamiliar and more exciting context.

Description and talk can also serve as an imaginative focus by the way in which they are used to place the looking into a different kind of context. Sometimes this can be achieved by simply asking the children to 'see' something on a different scale or from a different point of view – as in Year 5 when the children were studying 'Rasco and the Rats of Nihm' for their fiction-based project and were asked to surmise what the familiar world would look like through the eyes of a rat!

Changes of scale, context and meaning – whether achieved through looking or talking or both in harness, all help to transform the routine processes of observation and recording and to place them firmly within an expressive context.

Other important factors which help children to develop a variety of drawing skills are the ways teachers use time, scale and materials in association with looking and talking. A child in the reception class may make a perfectly satisfactory drawing in a few minutes especially when she is drawing from recall a familiar person or event. Five-year-olds need more time to make an observed drawing and this can engage them for as much as thirty minutes when the teacher makes good use of questioning to help them understand and 'see' what there is to be observed. As children move through the school, and as their drawing skills develop to enable them to make observations from complex source material, then much more time is needed for the drawing to be managed satisfactorily.

With older children time may be used and limited deliberately to encourage them to begin to use drawing to investigate possibilities. In Year 5, those children visiting the Beaford Centre in North Devon for the first time were confronted with a complex rural landscape. In order to help them make sense of what was there, they were asked to use their viewfinders like a photographer taking 'snapshots' and, in half an hour, to make at least four different drawings of parts of the landscape. Having to make these drawings very quickly encouraged them to seek essentials within the landscape and to consider alternative viewpoints and interests.

Children at Thornbury are well-supported in their work in drawing through the careful management of both materials and scale. It is very evident that children will approach a drawing task with much more confidence, especially in the early years, where the teacher has made a good match between the appearance and scale of that to be observed and the materials and scale of the drawing media to be used.

Initially, the teachers make these decisions and present the children with those drawing materials and papers of different shapes and sizes that correspond to the range of natural, manufactured and environmental resources which are used as starting points. Where the children are making studies from resources that are small scale and complex they will work on an appropriated scale and with such drawing media as biros, fine fibre-tipped pens or hard pencils so that they can manage the detail of what they are recording. Where studies are made from resources with strong colour or pattern qualities the children will work on a coloured ground and with pastels, or chalks or coloured pencils depending on the scale of that which is being observed.

Nearly all drawing tasks begin with some practice with the media to establish what it might achieve:

Fig. 5.11. Year 5. Using a view-finder to focus upon parts of the landscape.

Fig 5.12. Year 5. Four 'snap-shot' drawings of the Beaford landscape made in thirty minutes.

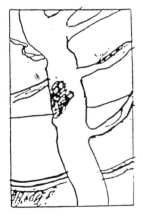

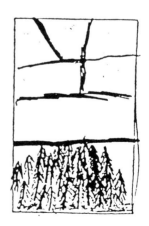

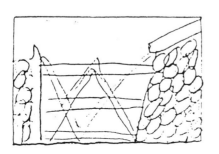

○ How many shades can you make with a 2B pencil?

○ How many different kinds of marks will a biro make?

○ How many different colours can you make with blue, green and black coloured pencils?

As the children progress through the school and become familiar with a full range of drawing media they increasingly make their own choices about what materials they might use. These choices are often the subject of serious discussion. The distribution and allocation of materials and equipment is rigorously organised throughout the school so that the children know exactly where they will find the resources they need.

The school's Art and Design Policy provides a detailed framework for the teaching of drawing and painting. Most importantly it describes those key elements that need to be taught and groups them in sequence so that staff can understand what children might achieve in Key Stage 1 and 2 and how their work with the children might be structured to support the development of these concepts.

The following extract describes how the teaching of the key concept of line within drawing is developed, what concepts should be taught within that context and with what supporting vocabulary.

Figs 5.13. and 5.14. Drawings from the environment and using a variety of pencils.

Contrasting uses of materials in response to working from different resources and starting points. All drawings from Year 5.

Fig 5.15. Study of houses. White chalk and crayon on black ground.

Fig 5.16. Plant Study. Pastels and crayons.

Fig 5.17. Landscape study in biro.

BROAD SKILL AREA	KEY ELEMENTS	IDEAS	VOCABULARY
LINE 5-7	1. The ability to identify the outline of natural and man made objects. 2. The ability to identify the concepts thick, thin, curved, straight, fast, slow. 3. The ability to use a variety of media to make a mark. 4. The ability to draw and isolate the outline of a natural/man made object. 5. The ability to change line direction. 6. The ability to use contour lines in a drawing. 7. The ability to identify the surface/contour of a shape/form.	- identifying a variety of outlines using overhead projector, strong light source to provide outline, silhouette etc. - using a varied vocabulary to describe a variety of lines identified by the children. - careful observation of natural/man made objects with a variety of outlines - discuss similarities and differences. - surface patterns - observation of line (implied) that gives texture. - discussion of variety of surfaces - natural.	outline silhouette telegraph lines pavement lines railway lines washing lines thick thin curved straight fast slow jagged
7-9	1. The ability to identify horizontal and vertical lines. 2. The ability to identify positive and negative. 3. The ability to do a blind contour drawing. 4. The ability to vary line thickness to suggest form and shadow. 5. The ability to use blocking in lines to emphasise angle and direction. 6. The ability to use sketch lines to suggest shape, texture and value.	- negative rubbings black crayon on white paper. - positive rubbings candle/white crayon on white paper with black wash. - use of natural surfaces for rubbings - small area for intense selection. - discussion and arrangement of rubbings. - experiment with B range of pencils: 1. hold in a variety of ways 2. use in a variety of ways. 3. test making and matching marks to the rubbings.	similar different gritty bumpy smooth lumpy surface rubbing variation form pattern
LINE 7-9	7. The ability to use gesture lines to suggest movement.	- variety of object e.g. bark, pebbles etc. and magnifying glass - close detailed observation. - repeat process of rubbing and comparison with - man made.	light dark regular, random pattern magnify
9-11	1. The ability to identify and use vertical, horizontal, diagonal and curved lines for direction. 2. The ability to identify line direction with associated objects. 3. The ability to see implied lines in a design.	- fill bottles/jars with string/pins/straws/pasta/coarse fabric - observation of patterns in the jar. - small viewfinder to select pattern - abstract and enlarge pattern - observing contour maps - the principle. - making contour map of a pebble, a thumb, a knee. - take irregular shapes and fill with linear contour lines. - use a variety of media. - change lines hard to soft, straight to wobbly etc.	man made viewfinder birds' eye view flattening represent contour biro, pencil, felt, charcoal/chalk

5.4. THE TRANSITION FROM DRAWING TO PAINTING

Children make a very similar transition in their use of painting to that already described in their work in drawing. Their first paintings, like their scribbles, are essentially playing with the media. Through this play they learn how to use paint, how to mix it, how to apply it and how to make in colour those simple symbols that represent for them familiar events in their own world. Their early paintings are very physical. They are a natural extension of their play with sand and water and where they enjoy the tactile sensation of pushing materials around!

As in their drawings, they paint symbolically and naturally as an extension to the story-telling through which they explain to themselves, to each other and to their teachers their response to a recent experience. They use colour arbitrarily and freely and without reference to colour in the real world. These early and unselfconscious paintings often have a magical quality about them because the child is 'reading' the world so spontaneously and directly.

At Thornbury, the children are encouraged and supported to use painting as a means of personal story-telling. At the same time, and alongside the way in which the staff support the children to embark upon descriptive drawing, they are given opportunities to explain their observations of the real world through painting.

In the Reception classes and in Year 1 it is quite natural for the children to paint spontaneously and symbolically one afternoon and to embark upon one of their early attempts at descriptive drawing or painting the following day.

As will be seen in the extract from the Art and Craft Policy below, this early play with colour is supported and structured through a variety of tasks that encourage the children to talk about and think about colour and to begin to use the special vocabulary of colour.

5.5. MAKING AND USING COLOUR

The key to all successful teaching of painting is to order the children's experience of making and using colour. As in the teaching of drawing from observation and analysis of the real world, the teaching of painting needs to be rooted in observation of real colour in the context of the children's world.

In their first paintings children will use colour arbitrarily. When they come to make their first paintings from things observed within the classroom — as for example, the first plants of the Spring, it is natural for the teacher to mix for them or to help them mix those colours they will need to paint the snowdrop or daffodil. They can then make that easy connection between colour observed and colours made.

When children begin to mix and make their own colours the range of colour is introduced simply and then adapted as the children progress with their colour making.

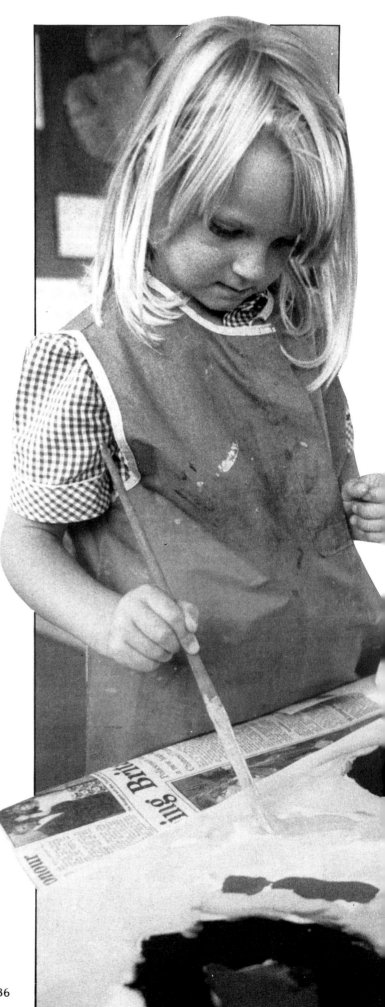

Fig 5.18. Reception class. 5 year-old enjoying an early painting.

36

The diagram below from the Art and Craft Policy explains the standard layout for the organisation of painting. Equipment and materials are so organised as to enable the children to make and use colour efficiently and the simple routine of using dry colour and water, palette and brushes is established early in the school.

As the children learn more about colour, the range is adjusted as follows:

RECOMMENDED ORGANISATION FOR PAINTING

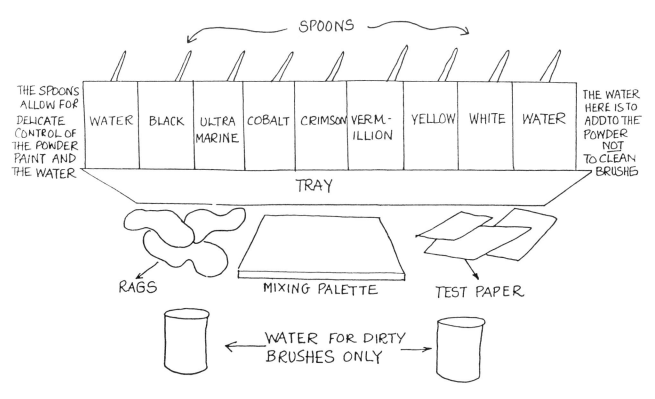

Fig 5.19. Recommended organisation for painting. From Art and Design Policy.

Fig 5.20. Year 1. A six year-old attempting his first painting in water colour.

(i) Black, Blue, Red, Yellow, White;

(ii) Blue, Vermilion, Crimson, Yellow, White;

(iii) Ultramarine, Cobalt, Vermilion, Crimson, Yellow, White.

Once the children have acquired sufficient knowledge about colour and the ability to handle the media effectively and with confidence and on the different scales that powder and water colour allow, then a more conscious and deliberate link can be made between drawing and painting. By the end of Key Stage 1 the children will be using painting as an extension of their drawing, particularly when working from environmental resources, and will begin by making a study in drawing before developing it further through making colour studies in other media (chalks, crayons, pastels) and then using the knowledge gained to pursue their ideas through painting.

Powder paint is used as the basic medium for all painting throughout the school because of the virtue it has of being a dry colour which has to be mixed with water to make a colour. This in itself encourages the children to consider and make colour carefully.

The use of water colour is introduced towards the end of Key Stage 1 and as soon as the children have sufficient control to handle colour on the smaller scale that water colour demands.

As may be noted from the Policy extracts, teaching colour is carefully structured to take the children logically through a number of stages in their understanding so that by the time they reach Year 6 they are able to deal with different aspects of colour under the headings:

    Primary and secondary colours

    Intermediate and related colours

    Value and intensity

    Harmony

    Monochromatic colour

Links are also established between the use of colour in painting and in craft areas such as weaving and batik (see Chapter 6 Designing and Making) or the Programme of Study 'Using Light' in the National Curriculum for Science.

BROAD SKILL AREA 5-7	KEY ELEMENTS	IDEAS	VOCABULARY
PRIMARY AND SECONDARY COLOURS	1. the ability to recognise the primary colours. 2. the ability to recognise the secondary colours. 3. the ability to mix the secondary colours. 4. the ability to 'mix' brown.	- a variety of situations that encourage playing with materials. - collecting, sorting, classifying with colours. - matching colour, colour word and collected objects.	red blue yellow primary violet green
VALUE AND INTENSITY	1. the ability to recognise light and dark primary and secondary colours. 2. the ability to use more than/less than in relation to light and dark colours. 3. the ability to recognise the neutrals - grey, black and white. 4. the ability to tone a primary/secondary colour and note the effect. 5. the ability to tint a primary/secondary colour and note the effect. 6. the ability to use the 'term' shade when observing tints and tones.	- colour mixing games - how many many can you make from the following. - favourite colours - magic quilt tints/tones of favourite colour. - building colour environments/displays. - changing light bulbs, spotlights, use of cellophane to create a colour view. - natural objects for children to observe and mix appropriate colour eg. leaves, bark, fruit, vegetables etc. - looking at transparent colour eg. cellophane, tissue, dye, brusho inks etc.	orange secondary colour match mix favourite tint tone shade change light transparent opaque observe media
HARMONY	1. the ability to relate feelings about colours. 2. the ability to give reasons why a colour is liked or disliked. 3. the ability to work from a limited palette. 4. the ability to experiment and choose colours that they think go 'well' together. 5. the ability to identify warm and cool colours.	- discussion of different effects by using a variety of pigments that 'add' colour. - original work of art that enhance colour observation (Colourists, Impressionists, Expressionists etc.) - using mixed media, collage, underlaying paint - graphic over - tooling.	choose Impressionist Expressionist Colourist black white grey neutral brown
MONO-CHROMATIC	1. the ability to work with black and white.		

BROAD SKILL AREA 7-9	KEY ELEMENTS	IDEAS	VOCABULARY
INTERMEDIATE AND RELATED COLOURS	1. the ability to recognise the intermediate colours 2. the ability to recognise the related colours. 3. the ability to mix the intermediate colours. 4. the ability to read the colour wheel.	- colour mixing games one colour adding a) yellow b) blue 3) black etc. Who can make most reds? - observing a display of one colour discussing variety of blues/reds etc. - working with one colour testing against a variety of backgrounds.	mix colour black white yellow etc. contrast
VALUE AND INTENSITY	1. the ability to discuss the tonal qualities created by light. 2. the ability to mix tones/tints. 3. the ability to understand the word 'value' and its effect on colour. 4. the ability to relate to the brightness/dullness of a colour.	- discussion of the variety of intermediate colours in works of art. - observational work of subject that requires good intermediate mixing skills eg. tomatoes on a purple and orange cloth. - colour charts (paint) ranging the pinks/oranges/browns/purples.	tone tint value bright dull compliment
HARMONY	1. the ability to identify complimentary colour colours. 2. the ability to observe the effect of the use of complimentary colour to produce vibrating sensations. 3. the ability to use related colours. 4. the ability to experiment with value change of warm and cool colours	- mixing from memory. - paint from observation and memory. - working with still life and primary colour and black and white eg. red apple/check cloth and red swathe.	vibrate warm/cool
MON-CHROMATIC	1. the ability to work with one primary colour and black and white.		

BROAD SKILL AREA 9-11	KEY ELEMENTS	IDEAS	VOCABULARY
COLOUR SOURCE	see Science Policy	- using pencil/charcoal/chalk to make value chart using three values - light, medium, dark. - repeat increasing value changes to 5 or 10.	light medium dark
VALUE AND INTESITY	1. the ability to change the tonal qualities using tint and shade. 2. the ability to change value qualities. 3. the ability to identify dark/light values and mix accordingly. 4. the ability to identify how tonal/value changes intensify. 5. the ability to identify how complimentary colour changes intensify.	- observing black/white photoes use of values. - observing artists work to note use of value changes. - select emotive words find and create colours that symbolize these words. - select variety of colours from magazines order them those that appear near-far etc.	value change tone tint shade harmony symbolize
HARMONY	1. the ability to identify three colour harmony. 2. the ability to work and mix three colour harmony. 3. the ability to identify and work in triadic harmony. 4. the ability to counter balance warm/cool colours.	- triad = 3 things/equally spaced eg. red, blue, yellow (see colour wheel) make posters. - observing how warm colours come forward cool colours recede. Paint in cool colours add small area of warm - what reaction. - from magazines select monochromatic, triad etc. harmonies.	contrasts triad distance nearness warm cool
MONO-CHROMATIC	1. the ability to interpret a set piece using primary/secondary or intermediate colour plus black and white.	- make a 5cm² colour swatch/or select from magazine - place in five other colour environments - observe effect.	forward recede

5.6. RESOURCES AND STARTING POINTS FOR PAINTING

The resources and starting points for working in painting are determined by those general principles that govern the use of resources in this school and which are described in Chapter 2. As in all other aspects of the curriculum, painting is used as another vehicle through which children can describe and respond to their own world and, of course, to the quality and richness of colour in the natural and made environment.

The full range of resources used in this school in 1989/90 is described in Appendix 1 (pages 118-128).

At Thornbury, once the children have moved beyond the stage of painting and drawing symbolically, all their work in painting is based upon investigation of the real world of colour in their environment or through using the work of other artists as an import-

ant focus for their own work in painting.

The descriptions of the teaching projects in Part 2 provide many good examples of the various ways that the environment is used as a stimulus to painting, ranging from symbolic paintings of the local playground by children in the Reception Class to sophisticated landscape paintings of North Devon and Dartmoor by children in years 5 and 6.

As the children move through the school, and once they have acquired those basic skills of making, describing and matching colour, an increasing use is made of references to the work of other painters to help them grasp the technical possibilities of painting and the variety of ways that colour may be used to explain and comment upon their experience of the world about them.

There is no doubt that children learn a great deal about painting by considering the way that other artists work. Their own response to the problems of painting a cityscape, a landscape, a still-life group or a

Fig 5.21. Year 2. Plant study. Drawing in crayons and pastels.

Fig 5.22. Year 2. Plant study in watercolour.

Fig 5.23.

Fig 5.24.

Year 2. Two landscape paintings in watercolour.
Illustrations for the fiction based topic 'Dragon Days'.

Fig 5.25. Monet's 'Water Lillies'.

Fig 5.26. Studies of water using crayons and pastels.

Fig 5.27. Study of colour in water using collage.

Fig 5.28. Watercolour, 'Water Lillies'.

Fig 5.29. Watercolour, 'Water Lillies'.

Fig 5.30. Watercolour, 'Water Lillies'.

Year 6. Eleven year- olds using paintings by Monet to generate their own paintings of water and ponds.

Year 4. The use of paintings by Henri Rousseau in association with a visit to Paignton Zoo to help children extend their understanding of the possibilities of making paintings of jungles.

Fig 5.31. Henri Rousseau.

Fig 5.32. 'Tiger'. Painting in watercolour.

Fig 5.33. 'The Hungry Lion'. Painting in watercolour.

Fig 5.34. 'Tiger'. Batik.

Fig 3.35. Group painting of a jungle made by the whole class working together.

Fig 5.35. Detail of group painting of jungle.

figure will be strengthened through the way in which teachers use references to the work of other artists to help children focus upon the possibilities of the task in hand.

At a very simple level, this focus may be achieved through encouraging the children to make mimetic paintings where they re- make or re-work another artist's painting and in that re-working they can learn much about the use of colour both descriptively and expressively.

The value of this way of working was particularly exemplified in the paintings made in response to the study of Monet's paintings at Giverney by children in Year 6.

More subtly, the work of other artists can be used to focus children's attention upon the possibilities presented when making a painting upon a particular theme or in response to certain environments. Where children are asked to make paintings of complex environments or demanding themes, it makes considerable sense for them to seek valuable clues to the various ways in which these demands might be addressed in the work of other artists. Otherwise they may be discouraged by the complexity of the painting problem and take consequent refuge in those familiar cliches that help them to avoid the real issue.

In this year at Thornbury, particularly good use was made by children in Year 4 of paintings by Henri Rousseau to help them respond effectively to a visit to the tropical house at Paignton Zoo and to see beyond the conventional cliche of 'The Jungle'. In Year 5, intensive use was made of paintings by artists of the Newlyn School to help the children to see the possibilities of a visit to the fishing port at Polperro in Cornwall. In Year 6 an exhibition of the work of Devon landscape painters was used to focus the children's attention upon the various ways they might respond to making paintings of the landscape of Dartmoor.

Listed below are the names of the artists whose work was used and those exhibitions seen in the school as reference and resource material in Key Stage 2 in 1988/89. This gives some indication of the way works of art are used in this school to enrich the children's painting in much the same way that a range of literature is used to help the children grasp the possibilities of language.

L. S. Lowry	Rothko
Mary Cassat	Rousseau
Van der Hooch	Cezanne
Vermeer	Pisarro
Frank Bramley	Seurat
Gwen John	Matisse
David Hockney	Beryl Cook
Van Gogh	Moore
Monet	Munch
Canaletto	Ernst
Whistler	Stanhope Forbes
Derain	Percy Craft
Breughel	Winslow Homer
Klee	Gorky
Constable	Beardsley
Monet	Dali
Sisley	De Chirico
Marquet	William Morris
Poussin	Turner
Uccello	Sutherland
Piero della Francesca	Paul Nash
Rackham	Walter Langley

Japanese Woodcuts
Illuminated lettering

Art Nouveau designers
Heraldic Designs

Exhibition 'Landscape and Colour in Devon'
Exhibition 'What is a Print'

DESIGNING AND MAKING

6.1. DESIGNING AND MAKING AS AN EXTENSION OF INVESTIGATION AND DRAWING

As in all other aspects of the Thornbury curriculum, designing and making take place in the context of real investigation and learning. The children are taught crafting and making skills in a variety of media. These skills are always used supportively to enable children to make what they need within the context of a particular task or project.

The context for designing and making, used within the school is similar to that described in the National Curriculum programmes of study in Technology. The teachers seek real designing and making tasks for the children within the context of Home, School, Environment, Recreation, Business and Community.

These contexts range from reconstructing favourite toys in the Reception class to a complex industry based project in Year 6 where the children formed a company to design, make, market and sell garden products through 'The Lazy Daisy Company' described in detail in Part 2 (pages 108 – 115).

All designing and making at Thornbury grows from investigation and through drawing. The initial drawing is used predominantly to familiarise the children with the content and detail of that artefact or environment that is to be explored through the designing and making. When the children are familiar with and confident about their understanding of the content, they are much better placed to focus upon the material and technical problems that are inherent to the different design and craft disciplines. This initial investigation, collecting information and making drawings from a range of natural and made resources is an essential part of Attainment Target 1 'Investigating Needs and Opportunities' in the National Curriculum documents for Technology.

6.2. DESIGNING AND MAKING IN THE EARLY YEARS.

In Chapter 3 the following statement summarises the importance to the children of their being involved with and excited by the problems of designing and making.

In working with materials, in learning how to shape and form both two and three dimensionally, children acquire and develop those making and handling skills that will form the basis for both craftsmanship and technical accomplishment.

Fig 6.2. Year 2. Drawings and models of 'The Iron Man'.

In the early years at Thornbury, in reception and in Years 1 and 2, the basis for these designing and making skills are established in a number of ways.

Initially, the children are encouraged to explore and use a variety of materials purposefully. Sand and water play, and playing with and using a variety of constructional units, are used positively to encourage the children to experiment, conjecture, invent, and attempt to come to decisions about what works and what does not through trial and error. All this work is richly reinforced through the use of language to challenge individuals and groups of children about what they are trying to do, what they are making, what does it mean to them and does it work!

They are encouraged to translate their drawings and their ideas into three dimensional form where this is appropriate. Can I make a reconstruction of my drawing of my teddy bear using the familiar range of junk materials? (figure 6.3).   What materials can I use to make the terrifying figure of 'The Iron Man' in Ted Hughes' story? (figure 6.2).   There is an over-riding concern here to ensure that these three-dimensional reconstructions are as well made as the drawings that describe them. The skills of cutting, folding, gluing and assembling are seriously addressed in order that the children not only gain pleasure from recreating a favourite image in three-dimensions, but gain satisfaction and pride from making them as well.

In these early years, much of the designing and making activity grows naturally from the desire to reconstruct or make in other materials images that have been observed, described, recollected or invented.

There is a similar approach to encouraging children

to design in two- dimensional materials. In Year 1 the children investigated and reconstructed in paper and card the different ways in which their coats and anoraks were constructed and their fastenings made effective, (figure 6.4). In Year 2 their drawings of their own hands were used as the starting point for designing gloves and mittens to cover them (figure 6.4 a & b). They used their investigation of the design of a Victorian christening gown to develop their own designs in Batik and, in their work related to the study of Roald Dahl's 'James and Giant Peach', they designed and made weavings based upon the subtle range of colours to be observed within peaches.

In the early years, the skills of designing and making are acquired as the need is determined by the nature of the enquiry. Only the basic skills in the handling of clay are taught separately and here, the teacher responsible for work in ceramics, teaches a programme of work in clay related to language enrichment and where all the work is linked to story telling and description within the class topic.

It is recognised that designing and making are time consuming activities and that in order to acquire good making skills and confidence in the handling of materials and techniques children need time to practice, to learn through their mistakes and to experiment. In order to make this time it is usual for only one craft and design area to be explored in each term in order that the children can focus upon a particular making activity. The detailed planning that supports the work at Thornbury and the cross-reference between year groups ensures that children receive a good range of designing and making opportunities as they move through the school.

6.3. DEVELOPING CRAFT AND DESIGN SKILLS

As in the teaching of drawing and painting, careful attention is given to the way in which the skills of designing and making are taught and in what sequence. The school's policy document provides a detailed framework for the teaching of those craft disciplines that are an essential support to designing and making.

In Key Stage 1, the making skills required are comparatively simple and are taught as they are needed to enable the children to translate their investigations and drawings into equivalents in other materials. In Key Stage 2 the making skills need to be taught more systematically and in such sequence that they move on to more demanding and complex problems of designing and making as they grow in confidence in their handling of one of the craft disciplines.

The extracts below from the Thornbury Art and Design Policy (figures 6.8 – 6.10) illustrate how the teaching of these making skills is implemented in the area of ceramics, weaving and printing.

The range of craft skills taught will vary from year to year depending upon the teaching skills and interests of staff within each of the year groups. Team teaching does allow individual teachers within each year group to lead particular craft projects across the year group and to act as consultants to other staff.

Teaching skills are reinforced through school based in-service workshops to provide staff with personal experience of working with different materials and so that they are familiar with the technical problems and opportunities each material will present to the children.

As the children move through the school and as they are presented with increasingly complex designing and making problems, an emphasis is placed upon their focusing their work within one particular designing discipline in each term. This ensures that they have sufficient time to develop their design ideas and bring them to a satisfactory solution both technically and aesthetically. It is recognised that children can only design and make effectively when they are given good quality tools and materials to work with.

In addition to providing a framework for teaching designing and making skills, the Art and Design Policy also contains technical information about particular methods and processes which may be used as for example in figure 6.11 below which illustrates basic techniques in weaving.

6.4. DESIGNING AND MAKING IN CONTEXT

Reference has already been made in 6.1. and 6.2. to the way in which designing and making are taught in different kinds of context in this school. In the early years, making is very much a three-dimensional extension of story- telling through which the children may reinforce their understanding of particular descriptions and content within their use of language. The context for their designing and making is thus a very personal one. In Years 1 and 2 this is gradually extended through using a variety of materials and techniques to encourage the children to investigate more specifically how familiar objects and artefacts are designed and made.

In this year in the school, in Key Stage 1, the children investigated and redesigned different kinds of spectacles, items of clothing, telephones, carry cots and toys.

In Years 3, 4, 5 and 6 this simple reconstruction of familiar artefacts and systems is extended further through presenting them with more specific problem solving tasks where they are required to consider not just the appearance of familiar artefacts and how they might be re- embellished, but also how such artefacts and systems work. And so they become engaged in considering such problems as:

○ Redesigning playground equipment.

○ How different kinds of bridges carry different loads.

○ What kind of vehicle is needed to cope with the rough terrain of Dartmoor.

○ Planning for the pedestrianisation of Plymouth City Centre.

○ Making a burglar alarm.

○ Designing and making environments to house rats, etc.

These contexts for designing and making in Key Stage 2 closely parallel those required within the programmes of study for Technology in the National Curriculum.

As the children move through the school there is also an increasing emphasis upon helping the children to understand how they might investigate and use familiar things within the environment as source material for designing and making.

In this particular year, children in Years 1 and 2 began by seeking out and recording the patterns in familiar clothes and the colours to be found in peaches to provide them with visual information to use in their own designs.

All the work in drawing and painting, where the children are taught to use the familiar language of the visual elements of colour, pattern, line, tone and surface, supports their work in designing and making.

The school's Art and Design Policy (figure 6.14) provides teachers with useful examples of how they can help children to investigate familiar things through analysing their appearance and extracting the information they need to support their designing and making in different craft disciplines. This process of observation, analysis and extraction of design information is best exemplified in the descriptions of the Year 6 projects on Dartmoor (pages 78 – 87) and the industry-based project on 'Gardens' (pages 108 – 115).

Fig 6.3. Reception Class. Reconstructions of teddy bears.

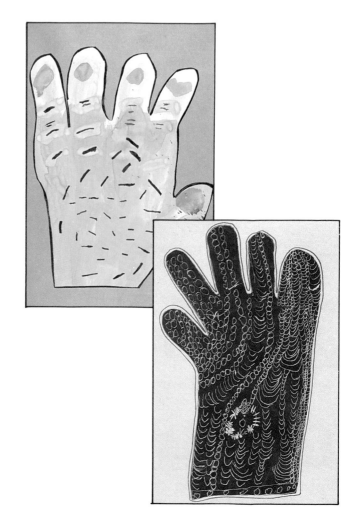

Fig 6.4.(a) Year 1. Drawing of own hand.

Fig 6.4.(b) Year 1. Design for a glove.

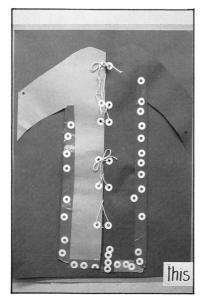

Fig 6.4. Year 1. Paper construction to explain how a duffle coat is fastened.

Fig 6.5. Year 2. Drawing of a victorian christening dress.

Fig 6.6. Year 2. Studies of patterns in christening dress.

Fig 6.7. Year 2. Batik design based upon christening dress studies.

Fig 6.8. Extract from Guidelines. Developments in ceramics.

CERAMICS	7 YEARS	9 YEARS	11 YEARS
	To be able to explore and discover the potential of clay. The ability to roll balls of clay of various sizes. The ability to coil clay of different lengths and thickness.. The ability to use balls and coils to create shapes and letters, wavy and straight lines. The ability to pinch small balls of clay into hollow 'pots' using pinch,turn method. The ability to tap clay against flat surface to create a cube. The ability to use 'scratch and slip' method to: a) join any of the elements together to create models of observed form. b) join coils to form small coil pots using supporting inner tube if necessary. c) join pellets, coils to flattened clay. The ability to devlop texture: a) using fingers, found objects - natural/man made, modelling tools to create marks. b) use small 'biscuits' of clay to explore environmental textures. c) to build relief pattern with coils and pellets. d) to cut out simple shapes adding pattern and texture. The awareness of technical points. The awareness of the firing process. The ability to prepare clay. The ability to use guides and rolling pins. The ability to use a pottery knife. The ability to develop linear patterns. The ability to work on large slab with group. The ability to understand the effect of firing.	The ability to plan and execute work. The ability to select the most apropriate method of construction. The ability to respond to thickness, weight, balance and surface. The ability to construct 3D forms, shapes and structures that are more complex. The ability to work on individual and group plaques. The ability to achieve effects relating to theme/ mood. The ability to build relief using coil, pellets and cut out shapes. The ability to use finer cutting skills to create space and light. The ability to use guides and rolling pins to create flat sheets of clay to use with convex forms and around tubes. The ability to understand and use coloured slips, underglaze colour and oxides. The ability to use correct terms and language at all times.	The ability to work with slip casting forms. The ability to show refinement and sensitivity in selecting the most appropriate means of achieving a particular effect. The ability to consider carefully the design of a plaque. The ability to build complex structures with slabs. The ability to use concave moulds as a basis for work. The ability to suggest solutions to technical problems that might arise. The ability to use wax resist and egraffito as a decorative technique. The ability to select personal decorative and glaze techniques. The ability to understand kiln loading. The ability to understand kiln firing.

Fig 6.9. Extract from Guidelines. Developments in weaving.

WEAVING	7 YEARS	9 YEARS	11 YEARS
	The ability to use a pair of scissors. The ability to understand the concepts of in and out/ under and over. The ability to weave paper ¼". The ability to weave rags/ material. The ability to cut the correct length of wool. The ability to thread a large eyed weaving needle. The ability to use the terms wool, loom, weave, through, across, push down, move up, tight and loose. The ability to thread wool in a weave on a small 1cm spaced cardboard loom. The ability to select and change colour. The ability to double thread wool for thickness. The ability to use fingers to weave. The ability to incorporate object - natural and man made. The ability to sort colours and tones.	The ability to use a larger cardboard loom. The ability to insert a beating board. The ability to weave straight, even lines. The ability to recognise faults and self correct. The ability to make 'openings' in weaving. The ability to weave the opening in contrast. The ability to weave wavy lines. The ability to increase blocks of weaving. The ability to decrease blocks of weaving. The ability to create different shapes. The ability to understand that weaving is basically a 2D form in a rigid frame. The ability to use subtle and accurate shading. The ability to experiment with shade and movement. The ability to maintain even edges. The ability to understand the terms warp, weft and tension. The ability to translate a design in shape and colour, sorting medium and limitations. The ability to combine technique, colour and additions of a 3D nature to enhance a design.	The ability to use a large wood framed loom. The ability to warp loom with correct tension. The ability to devise alternate looms. The ability to use wrapping technique. The ability to use looping technique. The ability to use knotting technique. The ability to use plaiting technique. The ability to use chaining technique. The ability to use sonmak technique. The ability to understand the effect of a variety of techniques and when it is suitable to use them. The ability to select loom, materials and technique to interpret a design. The ability to understand the process of wool. The ability to experiment with wool washing, dying, carding and hand spinning. The ability to understand larger looms and experience if possible.

Fig 6.10. Extract from Guidelines. Developments in print making.

PRINTING	7 YEARS	9 YEARS	11 YEARS
	The ability to use hands, fingers and feet to make a print. The ability to use a variety of natural objects to make a single print. The ability to use a variety of man made objects to make a single print. The ability to use man made and natural objects to make random prints in one colour. The ability to use two objects and two colours without mixing the colours. The ability to make successive prints in a straight line. The ability to make alternate prints. The ability to use press- print as a mono-print. The ability to etch a print in rolled ink. ALTHOUGH SILK SCREEN IS NOT HERE AS A SKILL THIS DOES NOT ELIMINATE ITS USE WITH YOUNGER CHILDREN.	The ability to successfully use objects to make successive prints and ½ drop prints. The ability to use objects that contrast a print e.g. 4 circles + overlaid star. The ability to compile a relief block using a variety of materials and successfully print. The ability to use press- print for overprinting. The ability to finely tool in ink and take a good print. The ability to organise tools for printing successfully. The ability to use torn paper for silk screen.	The ability to set up a silk screen for use and gather relevant materials. The ability to take a design through to a stencil. The ability to see positive shapes. The ability to see negative space. The ability to work on a single print building up to two colours. The ability to work on a simple repeat silk screen print using simple guide lines.

WEAVING

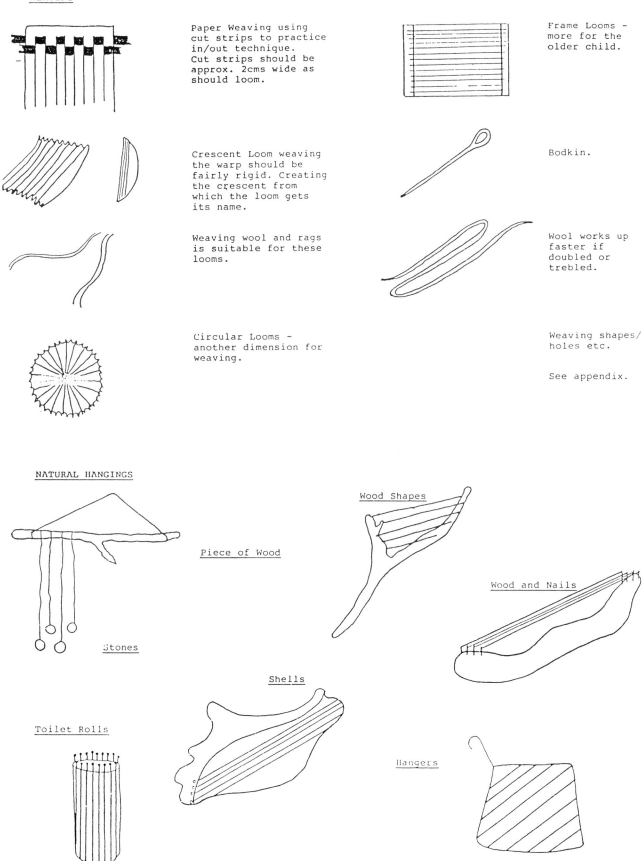

Paper Weaving using cut strips to practice in/out technique. Cut strips should be approx. 2cms wide as should loom.

Frame Looms - more for the older child.

Crescent Loom weaving the warp should be fairly rigid. Creating the crescent from which the loom gets its name.

Bodkin.

Weaving wool and rags is suitable for these looms.

Wool works up faster if doubled or trebled.

Circular Looms - another dimension for weaving.

Weaving shapes/ holes etc.

See appendix.

NATURAL HANGINGS

Wood Shapes

Piece of Wood

Wood and Nails

Stones

Shells

Toilet Rolls

Hangers

Fig 6.11. Extract from Guidelines. Weaving Techniques.

51

The teachers themselves have shared their enthusiasm for designing and making with the children by constructing for them environments within their teaching spaces that would serve as exciting starting points for their work in some of their teaching projects. For the fiction based projects 'James and the Giant Peach' and 'Dragon Days' (described on pages 88 – 100) the staff working with these year groups used a variety of materials to create the interior of the giant peach and Merlin's cave respectively. Both these environments served as important stimuli and a focus for the initial stages of work on these themes.

The school has a long tradition of presenting its work effectively and publicly. Considerable care is given to the way in which children's work is presented both within teaching bases and publicly throughout the school. The children's work is always presented in association with the reference material and resources that generated its thinking. In this way, and in the visual presentation of its work to the children and to visitors, the school makes an important statement to its community about the way in which it values and celebrates the work of the children.

From Key Stage 2, the children themselves are actively involved in the design and presentation of these public demonstrations of their work.

Fig 6.12. and 6.13. Year 4. Children making batiks.

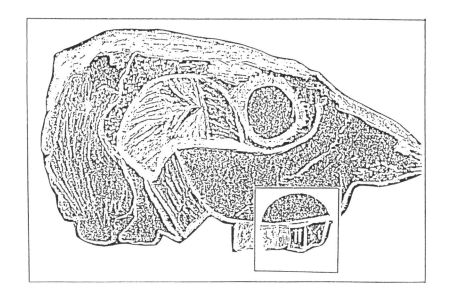

Age 11

Abstracting Design from an observed form

Stage 1 Close observation of a cow's skull using chalk, charcoal, pastel and conté sticks.

Stage 2 Key hole a section of your choice.

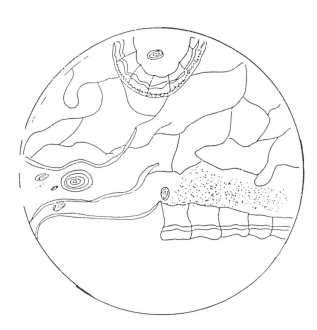

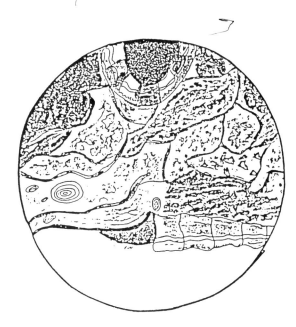

Stage 3 Abstract the Main lines using pencil and add any imaginative elements.

Stage 4 Add colour and texture using watercolour and inks

Stage 5 Create a relief in ceramics
or
create a padded embroidery
or
create a weaving

Fig 6.14. Extract from Guidelines. Analysing and selecting information through drawing.

Fig 6.15. Year 4. Making ceramic reliefs based upon studies of plants.

APPRAISAL AND ASSESSMENT

7.1. THE BEGINNINGS OF APPRAISAL: TALK AND REFLECTION

The single most important element of any curriculum is the development of the children's oral language through stimulating interactive discussion which immediately involves them in the development of their senses.

(Chapter 3, page 9)

The assessment of children's work in art and design is most naturally achieved when it grows out of talking to children about their own work. This form of self-appraisal by the child allows the teacher to gain access to some of the thinking and feeling that the child has brought to the work in response to the initial stimulus.

Because the use of oral language is so richly embedded in the curriculum at Thornbury, it is comparatively easy for the teachers to bring to their assessment of the children's work in art and design that same sense of sharing achievement through dialogue that is a characteristic of their approach across the curriculum. The assessment of achievement in art and design is negotiated between teacher and child and this dialogue enables the teacher to have insights into those processes and ideas that the child has brought to the making of an image or artefact.

When the children in Reception and in Years 1 and 2 are making their 'story telling' drawings, the teachers help them by listening to the commentary that so often accompanies the drawing and the children are challenged by suggestions for extensions to the drawing where this is appropriate.

Where the children are making their first drawings from observation, the dialogue between teacher and child will be simple and pragmatic and will be concerned with ways of looking carefully, ways of using materials and ways of making different effects with different materials. Some of these strategies have already been explored in Chapter 5.

The nature of the dialogue and of the talk that it might generate between children, as well as between teacher and child, will depend upon the kind of task to which the children have been asked to respond. Dialogue and discussion about drawing from observation is mainly concerned with looking – it is about using talk to enable the child to see what is there, to describe what they see, to speculate about how they might translate what they can describe and see into a drawing.

Discussion between teacher and child when the task is about making things will be mainly concerned with technical matters – it is about using and working with clay, fabric or paint in a particular kind of way. Dialogue between teacher and child will change dramatically when the task is open- ended and involves children in speculation, invention or recollection.

7.2. MATCH BETWEEN TASK AND ASSESSMENT

When, with the children, teachers at Thornbury assess work in art and design, they recognise how important it is to relate the assessment and talk closely to the nature of the task. They try to be as specific as possible as they seek the children's views about what they have achieved within the task. It is of little value to children for them to be told that their painting or construction is 'nice' or 'interesting' or 'quite good' or 'a bit careless'. Such generalised comments do little more than diminish the child's achievement. Where the task has been properly focused through the initial talk and discussion then dialogue and appraisal will follow naturally.

The extracts from the school's Art and Design Policy included in Chapters 4, 5 and 6, illustrate how carefully the work in art and design is structured to enable children to work with confidence through knowledge and understanding of the work they are engaged with.

Three aspects of the work at Thornbury make the crucial match between task and assessment more accessible:

○ all the work is based upon experiences that are shared between teacher and child and this in itself provides a natural platform for dialogue between teacher and child about the work in hand;

○ all technical aspects of the work – be it making colour, using a pencil, exploring surface, making a print etc, are methodically taught and in such a way as to support the children's enquiry and image making;

○ this approach is extended through the use of appropriate 'art' language so that the children can discuss their work with each other and with the teachers knowledgably and with a shared art vocabulary.

There is an understanding within the school of the different purposes for which art and design may be used within the curriculum. These are described in Chapter 4.3. Such shared understanding of the purpose of the task in which they are engaged provides a

Fig 7.1. Using viewfinders to study in detail Breughel's 'Childrens' Games'.

Figs 7.2. and 7.3. Year 5. Study from observation of 'V.E. Day, 1945' by L S Lowry.

secure base for negotiation between teacher and child about what has been achieved.

It is comparatively easy to assess with children what they have achieved where the work is concerned mainly with descriptions of things seen and shared with the teacher. Where the children are taking more initiatives and personal decisions themselves the tasks are more complex and personal and consequently the questioning and appraisal become more complex. Although much of what has been achieved will be evident in the work, there are some perceptions and responses that will contribute to the making that may not necessarily be evident in the final form. The kind of talk and the perceptions that inevitably emerge through discussions about work with both teacher and peers, often reveal qualities that are an important by-product of practical work in art and design. Such talk is not possible unless the children acquire through their work an art vocabulary that enables them to share their perceptions of their work with others.

7.3. USING CRITICAL STUDIES IN SUPPORT OF APPRAISAL

Through the rich use of evidence of the work of artists, designers and craft workers in association with their own work, the children come to a better understanding of the relationship between their own work in school and that in the world outside of school.

(Thornbury Art and Design Guidelines).

The use and development of work in critical studies has already been discussed in Chapter 3 where it is proposed that children can come to a better understanding of their own work through appraisal and use of the work of other artists. This is self-evident in the work at Thornbury Primary School where there has been a long tradition of using the work of artists and designers in much the same way as the work of writers is used in the school to give children access to a wider range of possibilities in their use of language.

Good examples of this practice are described in Chapter 3 where the visit to Exeter of an exhibition of work by L.S. Lowry was used to generate a detailed comparison of the contrasts between industrial and rural landscapes and, in Chapter 5, where paintings by Henri Rousseau and Claude Monet were used to enrich the children's work in painting.

There is an attempt within the school to develop a structured use of work in critical studies to match the children's developing perceptions of their own work. Initially, and with the younger children, there is a straightforward use of descriptive or 'mimetic' work where the children draw or paint their own versions of another artist's work which is relevant to the theme or topic they are pursuing. This has value in familiarising them with artist's work and with the variety of ways in which media may be used by artists to obtain particular effects. Evidence of the way that artists work is used more systematically as the children's grow in technical competence when they may begin to analyse the different systems that artists use. The study of the way artists use colour to determine space or mood, or the way artists use different drawing systems to gain different effects are all as valuable to the children's image making as their study of different writers use of vocabulary is valuable to their personal writing and story telling.

By the time that the children reach Years 5/6 many of them are able to begin to recognise through their own work in critical studies, that artists bring different interpretations to their perception of the world and that this can colour and determine how they themselves might respond to different kinds of experience. This is best illustrated in the work based on the study of Dartmoor by children in Year 6 which is described in Chapter 8.

In this project, because the children had access to the exhibition 'Landscape and Colour in Devon', they were able to use their own studies of the landscape of Dartmoor more personally and expressively. In viewing and appraising the work of a variety of landscape painters they were able to see possibilities which extended beyond simply describing the landscape.

All the various ways of using the work of artists and the accompanying discussion, writing and interpretation, add significantly to the children's ability to appraise and better understand their own achievements. The extracts below from the School's Art and Design Policy illustrate how critical studies can be used positively to extend the children's thinking about their work.

CRITICAL STUDIES

Critical studies work cannot be considered as 'second hand imagery'. Works of art and architecture and designed forms can be successfully used to stimulate children's interest and help the teacher in focusing the child's attention upon visual qualities in the environment. With primary age children the aim of the experience is not to develop good taste and discrimination, but to open up the whole world of active looking. Children can be encouraged to learn about the use of colour in their own work through rich critical studies experience; equally the expression of ideas and the promotion of self-evaluation in their own work can be heightened by a quality critical studies approach.

7.4. A FRAMEWORK FOR ASSESSMENT AND EVALUATION

Assessment of the children's work and evaluation of

Fig 7.4. Year 4. Study from memory of Vincent van Gogh's drawing 'Pollarded Birches with Shepherd'.

Fig 7.5. Vincent van Gogh 'Pollarded Birches with Shepherd'. 1884.

the effectiveness of the teaching in art and design are closely inter-woven within the school.

The display and presentation of the children's work around the school is one of the most immediate ways of valuing and appraising the children's work – especially where care is taken to ensure that the work of all the children is valued in this way. By presenting a good cross section of the children's work and by presenting it within the context of the resources that have generated the work, the teachers ensure that the work in art and design undertaken in association with each of the class themes is properly valued. The displays of children's work are also used both to record the development of their work as it progresses and to celebrate the range of their achievements at its conclusion. Such displays can highlight the fact that within their work in art and design the children can achieve a variety of equally appropriate solutions in response to the tasks they have addressed.

Each year, the staff celebrate these achievements by presenting for parents and governors an exhibition of the work produced by children in Year 5 in response to their residential experience at the Beaford Centre in North Devon. The children and their parents are invited to a 'Private View' at the school and where the work is professionally presented and catalogued.

Such concerns for appraising and valuing children's work, through questioning, discussion, matching assessment to task, and using critical studies to extend the children's understanding of their work, all contribute to a continuing evaluation by the teachers of the effectiveness of art and design work in the school.

At the end of each project or term the following questions may be asked about what the children have achieved within their work on the project. These questions may form a simple profile for the assessment of the children's work.

Has the work helped to develop:

○ powers of observation?

○ new perceptions?

○ use of skills?

○ use of media?

○ appraisal of their own work?

○ critical analysis of the work of others?

○ art vocabulary?

○ personal strengths?

In this work, the staff at Thornbury are supported both by the general principles laid down in the County Guidelines for work in Art, Craft and Design in Primary Schools and through the detailed and very professional guidelines for their work which have been formulated by the Curriculum Leader for Art and Design. These guidelines have emerged through detailed discussions with the staff. This is a very important element in all the work at Thornbury. When teachers are involved in policy making deci-

sions and in the formulation of such guidelines, they ultimately take ownership of the completed documents.

The following quotation, from the National Curriculum Task Group on Assessment and Testing report, summarises the constructive thinking attitude towards assessment and accompanying evaluation of their teaching that is a characteristic of the work in this school.

Assessment is at the heart of the process of promoting children's learning. It can promote a framework in which educational objectives may be set and pupil's progress charted and expressed. It can yield a base for planning the next educational steps in response to children's needs. By facilitating dialogue between teachers it can enhance professional skills and help the school as a whole to strengthen learning across the curriculum and throughout the age range.

It may be a useful post-script to note that when the children at Thornbury transfer to their neighbouring comprehensive school, they are immediately recognisable to the teaching staff in the art and design department for their ability to work confidently in the subject, for the purposeful way they go about their work and for their willingness to engage in discussion about their intentions.

PART TWO

DOCUMENTATION OF TEACHING PROJECTS

This section of the book contains in some depth descriptions of particular themes undertaken during the 1899/1989 Academic Year. This work took place when teachers were beginning to express concern about the confines of the National Curriculum:

○ Would there be enough time for everything?

○ Would assessment be a benefit or a burden?

○ Would the time spent on observing and recording the children's work eat into the quality of the learning process?

At Thornbury we found the answers were based in good practice. If a school already operates well-planned work, properly matched to children's needs, and carries out formative assessment and recording as part of managing children's learning then all that should be needed are minor adjustments. Many adjustments would involve looking at where work overlaps. For example, the links between science, technology, design and art are very important when looking at the amount of time available and how it might be used to the best advantage.

AUTUMN TERM 1988

ASPECTS OF SPIRAL 1

Reception
'Me and My Family'

Years 3 and 4
'Thornbury and its Community'

Year 5
'Plymouth as a City'

Year 6
'Dartmoor'

SPIRAL 1: Me and My Family

Year group: Reception Infants
No of children: 27
No of teachers: 1
Length of time: 10 weeks

The aim of the early part of the Autumn Term Spiral is to make the children aware that they are part of a family unit and then, in succeeding years, to make them more aware of themselves as individuals who belong to a wider community.

The project started with the children looking at large (A1) black and white photographs from the Education Resources Service. These photographs covered a whole range of age groups from babies to old people; they promoted discussions about who was the older or younger and how you could tell. This led to further discussions about who they lived with and who was in their family. It involved the children in making head and shoulder drawings of members of their family, in a wide variety of media: charcoal, pencil, chalk, oil, pastels, micro liner. It is a belief at this school that quality work demands quality materials, therefore children are taught to use a wide range of materials from the time they enter school. Subsequently the drawings were used to create very simple family trees and time lines. This work started from where the children were and moved backwards to make them aware that time had passed – very difficult mathematical and historical concepts for young children. The teacher helped the children by asking, 'Do you remember …

… when you were at Nursery School?

… when you were little?

… when you were a baby?'

Drama work was used to highlight the differences between their youth and their grandparents age. It was also the vehicle for looking at the different roles members of the families play, and here we saw some interesting stereotyping. Some children were really into: 'granny does the ironing', 'daddy mends the car', 'mummy cooks the tea'. In discussion they were not concerned that maybe daddy could cook the tea and mummy could mend the car

An exciting part of the project for the children was inviting their grandparents or 'adopted' grandparents to a tea party. The aim was to discuss their roles and to see what the grandparents remembered about the children growing up. It led to work about guests, invitations, what people wear to parties and most of all what they would like their visitors to eat; jelly, cakes and sandwiches seemed a good idea! The sandwiches were all shapes and sizes as various mathematical patterns were tried out and the cake decorations showed definite imaginative flair.

The party was a great success and the grandparents commented most on the illustrated invitations they had received. Before they made these the children looked at a whole range of invitations, discussed their design, which ones they liked best and why. They had perused calligraphy books and books with illuminated letters, and compared these to the handwriting scheme which they were used to using. The depth of their research was reflected in the end product. It highlighted yet again the importance of real and relevant experience and the opportunities to talk about it. This approach encourages the teacher to direct young children's attention to detail by asking precise but open- ended questions.

The next two weeks of the project were spent visiting the local church – first for a christening and then for a wedding. On each occasion the children were appropriately dressed and played their assigned roles. Some of the children sketched the tableaux in situ and back at school turned the sketches into large paintings. At the end of the project the children had a good understanding not only of families but of the word 'celebration'.

It was an ideal time to explore this project because it led naturally into Christmas and the Nativity and helped to add depth to the children's understanding of this occasion.

NAME OF THEME It's Me   YEAR Reception   SPIRAL 1 AUTUMN TERM 1988
2 SPRING TERM 19
3 SUMMER TERM 19

AIMS

① To encourage the children to co-operate within a group situation.
② To extend the children's awareness & knowledge of themselves as part of their family, as individuals & as part of their class group.
③ To develop the children's oral language & their ability to discuss & listen to others.
④ To promote the children's ability in design & construction.
⑤ To give the children a greater awareness of their homes & houses in general.

OBJECTIVES

① To develop the children's ability to use equipment properly eg structured play, art equipment.
② To promote an awareness of their bodies & how they work.
③ To give understanding of present, past & future & the relevant vocabulary of time.
④ To give the children an awareness of people & time before they were born eg parents marrying, grandparents when they were young.
⑤ To encourage the children to explore their feelings & familiar roles through drama.
⑥ To be able to devise simple tests & predict outcomes.
⑦ To promote close observation eg through careful drawing.

RESOURCES visits, people, artefacts, community contacts, poems, stories, records

Visits - Christ Church, Estover
           Plymbridge Nursery

Visitors - The children's grandparents   A mother & baby
            The health visitor

Museum Service - Pictures of old people

Artefacts - Family photographs, clothes/toys belonging to the children when they were younger.

Stories/Poems - Avocado Baby, Grandpa & Me, Bible stories, Dogger, Goodnight Owl,
Poems from 'A kiss on the nose' by Tony Bradman
'This little Puffin'-Songs, number rhymes & finger plays

CONCEPTS
Change   Continuity & change
Communication   Stewardship
Similarity & difference

EVALUATION

Fig 8.1. Planning Sheet. Stage 1.

63

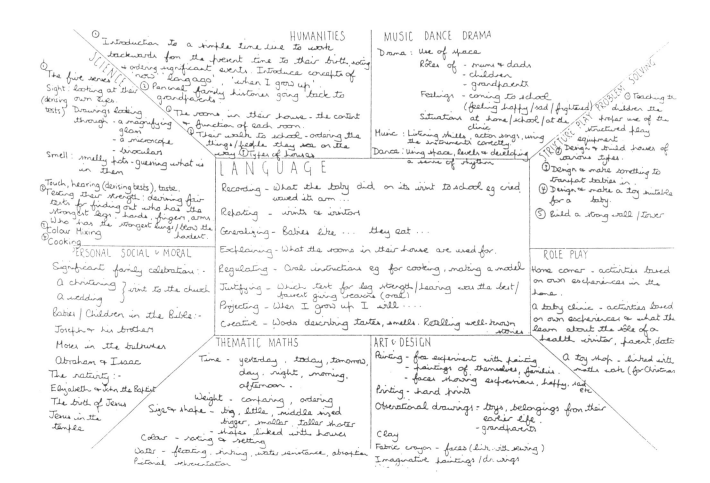

Fig 8.2. Planning Sheet. Stage 2

Fig 8.3 Display of photographs of grandparents.

Fig 8.4. Display of photographs of grandparents.

This theme moves out from the family to encompass where people live and what makes a community.

The children in Year 3 looked specifically at houses and homes and addressed such issues as:

○ 'What makes a home?'

○ 'Should we go on building houses on all the available land?'

○ 'Has everyone got somewhere to live?'

They looked particularly at the technological and design aspects of building a place to live:

○ 'What do we need to consider?'

○ 'How important are the aesthetics of it all?'

The children designed curtain and wallpaper fabrics and made a variety of blinds with different mechanisms for the south side of the classroom. This work lays a firm foundation for the work in Year 4 which is illustrated later in this section. At this stage the children address the wider issues of the community. In the Autumn Term of 1988 the work on the community commenced with a study of the school:

○ 'What is its value to the community?'

○ 'Where is it situated on the estate?'

○ 'Who works there?'

One of the aims of the project was to encourage in the children a caring attitude towards their environment. The first two weeks were spent looking at the design of the building and the school conservation area. The children drew birds' eye views of their journeys to and from the conservation area and they made detailed drawings of what they saw there. They then went out into the local area and visited the hospital, airport, church, and supermarket. They looked at the different organisations within these buildings and drew the various routes between them and the school. While on site they did quick sketches which were 'worked up' in various media on return to school.

A survey of the leisure activities in the area was carried out and provision was found to be sparse. This lead to a discussion about what should be available. Breughel's 'Children's Games' was used to promote their first idea of more play areas. They designed and made working models of a playground using everything from Fischer Technic to Lego.

All this work was supported by people from the community, visiting school and sharing their experiences with the children. One of the most successful visitors was an officer from the Town Planning Department, who really fired the children's imaginations when he explained to them the process of building the estate in which they now lived. They were not backward in pointing out to him the lack of leisure facilities or the fact that there were too many people for the various facilities provided! This exchange highlighted the value that work in oral language has for the children in giving them confidence to engage in debate.

Fig 8.5. Paintings of Grannies.

Fig 8.6. Paintings of ourselves playing in the park.

SPIRAL 1: Thornbury and its Community

Year group: 3 and 4 – Lower Junior
Number of children: 125
Number of teachers: 4
Length of time: 8 weeks

This theme moves out from the family to encompass where people live and what makes a community.

The children in Year 3 looked specifically at houses and homes and addressed such issues as:

○ 'What makes a home?'

○ 'Should we go on building houses on all the available land?'

○ 'Has everyone got somewhere to live?'

They looked particularly at the technological and design aspects of building a place to live:

○ 'What do we need to consider?'

○ 'How important are the aesthetics of it all?'

The children designed curtain and wallpaper fabrics and made a variety of blinds with different mechanisms for the south side of the classroom. This work lays a firm foundation for the work in Year 4 which is illustrated later in this section. At this stage the children address the wider issues of the community. In the Autumn Term of 1988 the work on the community commenced with a study of the school:

○ 'What is its value to the community?'

○ 'Where is it situated on the estate?'

One of the aims of the project was to encourage in the children a caring attitude towards their environment. The first two weeks were spent looking at the design of the building and the school conservation area. The children drew birds' eye views of their journeys to and from the conservation area and they made detailed drawings of what they saw there. They then went out into the local area and visited the hospital, airport, church, and supermarket. They looked at the different organisations within these buildings and drew the various routes between them and the school. While on site they did quick sketches which were 'worked up' in various media on return to school.

A survey of the leisure activities in the area was carried out and provision was found to be sparse. This lead to a discussion about what should be available. Breughel's 'Children's Games' was used to promote their first idea of more play areas. They designed and made working models of a playground using everything from Fischer Technic to Lego.

All this work was supported by people from the community, visiting school and sharing their experiences with the children. One of the most successful visitors was an officer from the Town Planning Department, who really fired the children's imaginations when he explained to them the process of building the estate in which they now lived. They were not backward in pointing out to him the lack of leisure facilities or the fact that there were too many people for the various facilities provided! This exchange highlighted the value that work in oral language has for the children in giving them confidence to engage in debate.

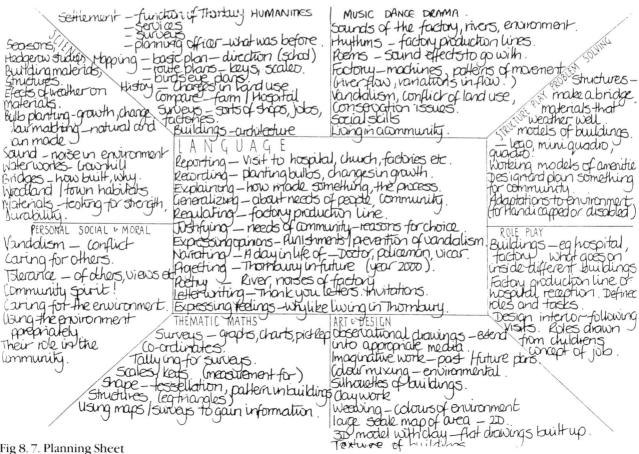

Fig 8. 7. Planning Sheet

	Week 1 & 2	Week 3 & 4	Week 5 & 6	Week 7 & 8
STIMULUS	The School (Dick Mayhew)	Airport, Hospital, Asda, Factory }1 group to each.	Leisure — park, Fursdon, Majons, clubs.	Dick Mayhew Plymbridge (planning officer)
Language Oral	People who work at school — interviewing discussing roles, Daily routines, Reporting.	Interviewing — developing questions before visit	What do you think of the facilities? What would you change?	Debate — housing, land use. Empathy comparison with other areas - school places of work
Language Written	A day in the life of ___ Reporting interviews	Thankyou letters. Regulating — factory process, shopping. Expressing opinion — land conflict	Expressing opinion — amenities Imaginative — what I would like	Describing what have seen Justifying, arguing persuading — need for areas to stay.
Poetry	Alan Aldberg — poem as stimulus Poems about people at school.			natural sounds — compare with school. River poems.
Drama	Peoples jobs, roles in school.	Land conflict, use of land.	Vandalism — caring for facilities (Policeman?)	Fools Theatre stimulate debate re: building on land where parts is now.
History	Development of the school — time line of photographs showing change.	Change to land use & buildings.		Comparative settlement railway, quarry.
Geography	Basic plans routes around school Direction Birdseye view	who works there, what people do. Position in relation to school.	Position in relation to settlement needs Population — figures and changes.	Conservation — position
P.S.M.	Groupings — class, school, community Common factors School rules.	Roles in the community.	Rules in community church Cultures — catering for peoples needs	Conservation, community spirit
Science	Conservation area — seed dispersal observation →	flight — testing	Fitness — health machines.	Bridges — testing structure
C.D.T. / Problem Solving		Flight.	Park, playground facilities — see-saw, roundabout, slide.	Bridges — Design and build — David Jinks wood
Art & Design	Observational drawing of school areas Views from window Improvements to school	Landscapes Observation on site 3D models Sequences.	Design park area. Sequence of line drawings showing movement	Colours, dying, weaving water movement shadows, textures natural studies.
Thematic Maths	Groups, settings graphs, Venn diag Statistics. Tessellation.	Surveys graphs, charts, tallying.	Graphs-fitness (capacity /volume (pool) money Tallying — usage. Timetabling — bus.	Symmetry, shape, area Pattern
Dance	Poem — Sounds at school (as music) Movement links Direction, pathways	Movement in flight, factory (machines, sequence)	Direction - movement of park facilities sequence. Percussion instruments.	River movement, changes in flow Percussion
Music	Sounds around school, in school Poem/sounds around school Add	Words to describe movements at each site. Link with sounds	music for mood eg relaxing, exercising rhythms to create	River flow movement of trees, noises around

Fig 8.8. Weekly record of work.

68

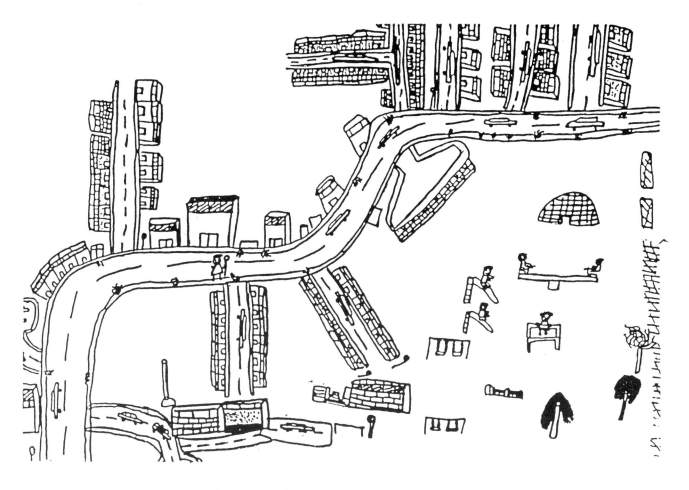

Fig 8.9. Year 3. Journey to School (micro-liner).

Fig 8.10. Year 3. Views about the school (pencil).

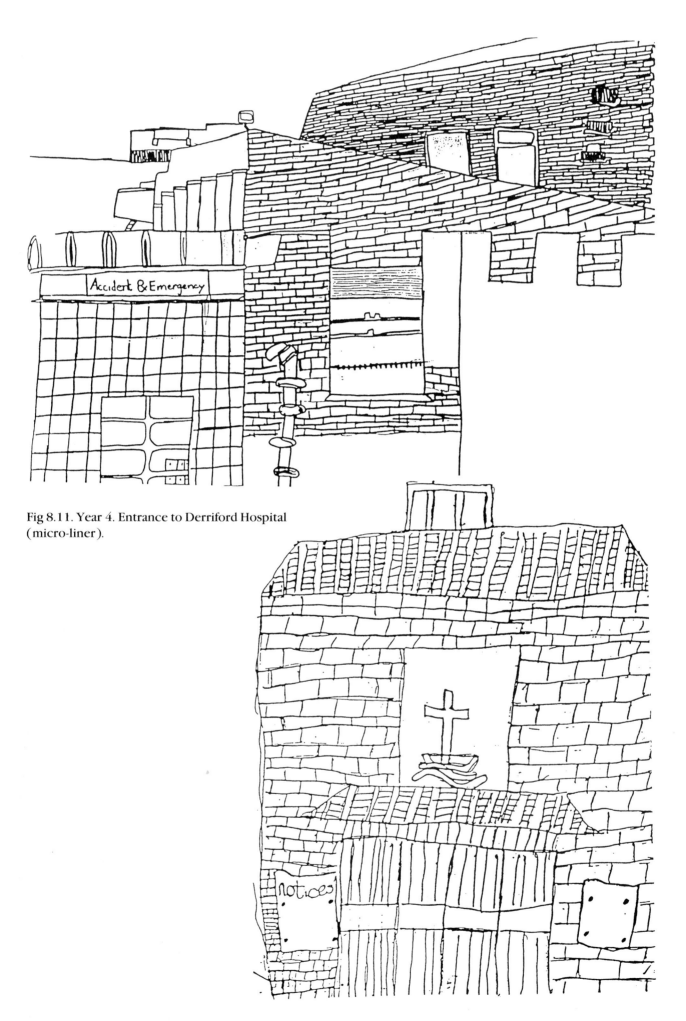

Fig 8.11. Year 4. Entrance to Derriford Hospital (micro-liner).

Fig 8.12. Year 4. Thornbury Church (pencil).

Fig 8.13. Year 4. Church fittings (mixed media).

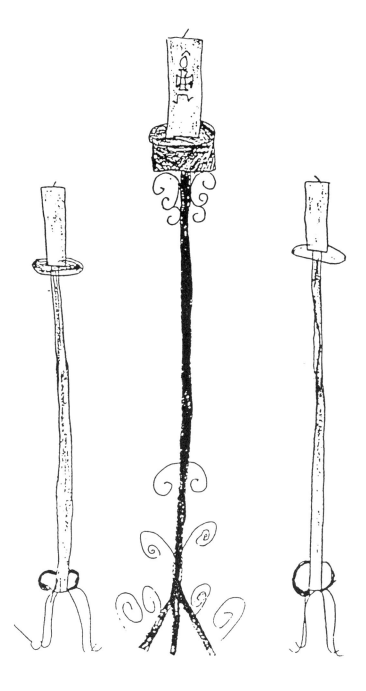

SPIRAL 1: Plymouth as a City

Year group: 5
Number of children: 88
Number of teachers: 3
Length of time: 8 weeks

The aim of this theme was to extend the children's learning about Thornbury and its place in the context of a wider community – the City of Plymouth. It was organised in five modules and commenced with two visits to the city centre. The discussion, close observation and drawing which took place on these visits heightened the children's awareness of the differences between the new and the old buildings.

The work produced in response to these experiences shows evidence of the depth of these discussions. Practically all the drawing took place in situ and the children were asked to move from making accurate detailed drawings of the buildings to creating their own imaginative cityscapes through their drawings. Reference was made to paintings by Klee and Lowry to reinforce this transition from observed to imaginative drawing. Back at school this work was used as a basis for further development in ceramics and soft fabrics.

The second module was introduced in a drama lesson which had as its starting point a discussion about the drawing 'Four Grey Sleepers' by Henry Moore. The aim of the lesson was to make the children aware of the evacuation of children in the Second World War. They already understood about the blitz and the reasons why so much of Plymouth had been rebuilt. The discussions about the 'Four Grey Sleepers' helped them to empathise with what it must have been like in air raid shelters and the need to move to a safer environment. All this work was well-supported by photographs, diaries and copies of log books from the local newspaper office.

The next module of work involved the children working with Chris Robinson, a local artist, who draws and paints water colours of Plymouth. He came to school to share with them his perceptions of the growth of the City. The children visited his studio and tried to produce work in a similar vein. Year 5 looked particularly at his work on local bridges and used this as a basis for constructing and testing their own bridges.

The fourth module included a visit to the Lord Mayor's Parlour to meet the Lord Mayor and find out how a city is run. Before the visit a questionnaire was constructed and tested and a great deal of discussion took place about the interview techniques. The visit raised the issue of the rights of the citizens and the importance of community life. The Lord Mayor wanted to know what they thought Plymouth would look like in twenty years time – so they wrote and told him!

The final module looked at Plymouth as a port. The children established what made a port and what type of advertising was necessary to attract people to use it. They experimented with poster making techniques, a video camera and 'jingles' made by using a tape recorder and improvised music. The whole issue of preference and how communication takes place was discussed.

The overall aim of the project was achieved – to give children an understanding of their role in the wider community of the city. It raised for them and for the teacher such issues as:

○ 'What makes a good citizen?'

○ 'What do we understand by community?'

○ 'Have we a sense of history?'

○ 'How do we acquire a set of values?'

The children's answers to these questions revealed some depth of understanding.

NAME OF THEME Plymouth   YEAR **5**   SPIRAL
1. AUTUMN TERM 1988
2. SPRING TERM 19
3. SUMMER TERM 19

AIMS

1. To extend the children's awareness of their environment.

2. To build on the children's concepts and skills & develop new ones.

3. To introduce the children to media studies

4. To build up a sense of identity with the wider community.

RESOURCES visits, people, artefacts, community contacts, poems, stories, records

Len Copley – ref city walks.
Crispin Gill – Plymouth historian
Chris Robinson (Artist & his book)
Dick Mayhew (Majorkas)
City Library & Museum
Library Service
Museum Service
W. Devon Records Office
Saltram House
Plymouth Airport / Station (rail / bus)
Town planner
Plymouth Tourist Board
Department Stores in City Centre.

Civic Centre/Lord Mayors Parlour
Cattedown Caves
Freedom Park
Q. Anne Battery
Plymouth Breakwater
Morning News / Herald / T.W.
Sealed Knot

OBJECTIVES

1. To extend the ideas of the Thornbury project to the city of Plymouth (community, belonging, responsibility etc.)
2. To develop the children's concept of the city they live in – Plymouth
3. To develop skills of synthesis and communication, orientation, geographical, critical appreciation, analysis and problem solving
4. To develop independent study skills.
5. To look critically at the resources in Plymouth and interpret them just a relevant manner thoughts about them

CONCEPTS

Change   Power
Stewardship   Conflict / Consensus
Cause / Effect Change
Communication

EVALUATION.

Mapping – geographical position Plymouth/ Devon/Britain HUMANITIES
Travel/Communication – trains/ferries/airport/routes
Street maps & patterns
Town "turning"   Facilities for – leisure
Town planning – now in the future sports
                                    theatre etc.
Timeline work – Pilgrim Fathers – Saltram – Brunel
  – the Blitz – the future.   local
Street & pub names   Papers/TV etc.
How is Plymouth run – civics
Plymouth the port – naval
Shops in the past v. stores commercial
                             recreational

SCIENCE
Structures (bridges etc.)
Tunnels
Ferries
Pulleys/cranes/weights
Mast (submarines etc.)
Where does Plymouth's water come from? – gas – electricity
People movers
Burglar alarms.

MUSIC DANCE DRAMA

Songs connected with the sea / Plymouth's history/bridges
Exploring the problems of pedestrianisation from different perspectives.
Communication through movement & music.
Stealthy movements – Burglary
Story put to music
Shop mannequins coming alive
Communicating with each other formal
a sequence of movements – body contact –
lines e.g. bridges
Drama/roles from history of Plymouth

STRUCTURE PLAY PROBLEM SOLVING
Town planning
 & pedestrianisation
Leisure complexe
what is Park planning.
needed? Shopping centre
How do we
provide it?
People movers
Burglar alarms.
Ferries (across the swimming pool?)

LANGUAGE

The language of the media.
Recording/reporting . . . . . . Visits/visitors/media reporting
Generalising . . . . comparisons/ data interpretation
Explaining . . . . describing the city to someone else,
                        giving directions, routes etc.
Expressing opinions . . . . . commenting on current affairs
Regulating . . . . ordering stages of an experiment
Justifying/Arguing/Persuading . . . should we move Derry's Clock?
Speculating . . . . if Plymouth didn't have a national
                        harbour what would it be like.
Projecting . . . . what will Plymouth be like in the future
Narrating . . . . stories from local events/history
Expressing feelings . . . . . empathy with other inhabitants
Letter writing/ . . . . . to a penpal from a 'twinned' town

PERSONAL SOCIAL & MORAL

Law and Order/Neighbourhood Watch/community care.
Vandalism v. looking after where we live
{Religious communities} Multicultural units within Plymouth.
How did communities begin?

ROLE PLAY

The Council "contemplate" problems
Pilgrim Fathers Talk mode via day council – how much has changed?
Plymouth Information Bus
"Dress" the Shop Window.

THEMATIC MATHS

Surveys – recording statistics etc.
e.g. Shopping, traffic, census figures etc.
Grids/Enlargements.
Coordinates
Timetables
Speed/distance work.

ART & DESIGN

Plymouth collage
Media studies – 'advertising' Plymouth
Designing logos
Designing ferry uniforms etc.
Drawings/paintings/models.

Fig 8.14. Planning Sheets.

STIMULUS	Visit to City Centre			Chris Robinson's work
Language Oral / Media	Establishing basic vocabulary eg. coast port, city, county, country. Use of photos/maps for discussion. Interviewing — Advert. Brainstorming →	→ **Level 3 Att 1.** → Media →	Discussion of worms eye view in conservation area (introd. 5/9) to be developed into Media → **Level 3**	Vocabulary for bridges, arched, suspension etc. Sharing ideas for media.
Language Written / media	"Plymouth is....." Reports of visit e aspect they've looked at in groups. Media Studies →	Use of 4 grey sleepers to promote poetry e creative writing about Blitz. Comparisons, observations, and conclusions from surveys, charts etc.	Worm's eye view of Plymouth. Reports of Visits Media →	Reports - testing brid Research skills for Brunel e bridges. →
Poetry	Plymouth - poetry written on this city or parts of it.	Blitz poetry/war 'Alive Poetry '85' feelings p85 War p93-104	'Thoughtshapes' 'Strange Worlds' p7 'Ruins e Remains' sections.	Cities 'second Poetry BK'. p108 Bird's eye vi Delights e Warning Parks p96 Demolition p66
Drama	Evacuation Why? How? Where to? How do you feel?	Evacuation →	Evacuation ? →	Civil War Work The battle of Freedom Fields.
History	Street names and place names	The Blitz. Att 5. Photos/diaries log books. Changing face of Plymouth as a result	(Detail) **Att 2.** Level 3 **Reading II** →	Tamar Bridge Brunel's Railway Bridge
Geography	zones of Plymouth and community areas	Orientation skills - tasks about moving from one area of Plymouth to another - directions	→	Grid work and changing scale.
P.S.M.	"Origins" - Plymouth Giants wrestling match (folklore)	"origins" - other Stories of creation →	**Att 3 Level 3-5**	Founders/Leaders e prophets eg. Gandhi
Science	Structures - strong shapes/buildings. **Att 1. Att** → Att 6. (Detail) →	Structures continued - tests on weight - bearing Att 10 level 5	Design own strong structures (Detail)	Building bridges e arches - testing their strength. Level 4.
C.D.T./Problem Solving Att 1.	Own plan for pedestrianisation of City Centre. Att →	Att 14. Level 3 Burglar alarms Att 11. level 3,4	Collapsing shelves Display materials for Sainsburys. →	
Art e Design	Sketching/collecting information. General observation work. Shop windows. Collage - on-going	Paintings of buildings 3D modelling of buildings. Mimetic Studies eg Lowry	Imaginary landscapes Worm's eye view 3D modelling contd. (b) Klee	Line drawings Printing of skyline e monoprints/ poly prints Pub signs.
Thematic Maths	Shopping survey. Graphs.	Graphs/Statistics Traffic census.	Graphs e Statistics Jobs e Employment. →	
Dance	Movement for communication Introduction. contact/non contact.	Security - moving Stealthily - "The Burglary" set to music	Extension 'Burglary' groups creating own music/movements using percussion instrum.	Civil War - linking story to movement

Fig 8.15. Weekly record of work.

	Week 10.10.88	Week 17.10.88	Week 31.10.88	Week 7.11.88
STIMULUS	Communications How the city is run Visit Lord Mayor's Parlour.		Visit Ferry/ Dockyard	
Language Att.1. Oral Level, 4,5?	Discussing how city operates. ? → Media	Debating local issues eg. pedestrianisation Giving oral directions Att 5. Level 5(c)	Language of headlines, slogans →	Sharing time for designs, paintings and future ideas for Plymouth.
Language Att 3 Written Levels 3-5	'The Diary of a Pilgrim Father' Part 1. 'The Groups I belong to' media	→ Part 2 ? - (setting up colony.)	Accounts of visits Ferry/ Dockyard in newspaper form.	'My View of Plymouth in Year 2010.'
Poetry	Att 12. Level 3 (computer)			
Drama	The Pilgrim Fathers —	Att 2 → Reading II	Setting up motte and Bailey castle. →	→
History	Pilgrim Fathers. →		Timeline - boats used in dockyard. Privatisation/recent history of the Dockyard.	Plymouth Defence
Geography	Grid work and changing scale.	Bus routes around Plymouth. Road routes in/ around city.	Orientation in relation to Plymouth & further by rail/road/air sea.	Looking at the map how far will Plymo spread in the future?
P.S.M.	Groups they belong to in the Community.	Famous people who have "given"/"give" to others eg. Mother Theresa, Father Damion, Martin Luther King.	Symbols - Christian and others.	Visit to the synagog Discussion of othe Churches. (Build-up to Xmas)
Science	Bridges testing/building weight - bearing.	Bridges. Comparing/contrasting different strengths weight - bearing experiments	Designing, making ferries & cranes Att 13 Level 3 level 4	→
C.D.T. / Problem Solving			Designing Plymouth for the future small groups eg. playground equipment problem - leisure centres Att 16 solving skipping areas.) Level 3 activities	
Art & Design	Logos for shops and travelling Collage -ongoing	Lowry - coming home from the Mill. —" Coming home from the Dockyard" People -scenes	Posters/ Advertising Plymouth 3D models →	→
Thematic Maths		Time table work - 24 hr clock - bus → - air - rail		
Dance	Communicating visual concepts shop displays, mannequins 'coming alive'	Extension set to music small groups creating own sequences.	Communicating with friends building cranes bulldozers/ human bridges in groups.	Extension - to larger groups set to own music
Music				

Fig 8.16. Weekly record of work.

Figs 8.17. & 8.18. Year 5. Studies of Derry's Cross.

Fig 8.19. City Centre Study.

Fig 8.20. Year 5. Studies of City Centre.

Fig 8.21. Year 5. Plymouth of the future. Speculative
drawings about Plymouth's future developments.

SPIRAL 1: Dartmoor

Year group: 6
Number of children: 105
Number of teachers: 3
Length of time: 8 weeks

For children in Year 6 this is the final unit of work on the Autumn Term Spiral. Each year the child's circle of knowledge has been increased and previous work consolidated. If Year 6 turns out to be a particularly mature group, 'Dartmoor' is replaced with a wider theme 'Family of Man', which is a comparative study of how they live compared to people in developing countries. In this particular autumn term, however, Year 6 studied Dartmoor.

The project started with a visit to part of Bellever Forest where, at the foot of the Tor, the East Dart river runs through the woods. The main aims of the project were to make children aware of the differences between this environment and their particularly urban environment and to draw their attention to the geological and geographical uniqueness of Dartmoor.

On site work at Bellever consisted of using large scale maps to identify the landscape and the main features within it. It included on the spot drama work and observational drawings which not only showed colour, tone and texture, but balance, rhythm and atmosphere. It raised issues such as how do people move around such a difficult terrain and this set the scene for designing, making and testing multi-terrain

vehicles. The scope of work from a well-chosen visit cannot be emphasised highly enough.

On their return to school the quality of the landscape was further highlighted by reference to the exhibition 'Landscape and Colour in Devon' which illustrates how different artists have responded to the shapes, colours and divisions of the landscape. Some of the children's most exciting paintings emerged from the combination of using this exhibition and the real experience of the landscape of Dartmoor.

The next part of the project involved the majority of the year group in a week's residential visit to Dartmoor. This added depth to the work mentioned in the previous paragraphs. It led particularly to a study of the movement of water which was consolidated through critical studies work using paintings by Turner, the Impressionists and the Fauves. It also set the scene for the next unit of work – Dartmoor Myths and Legends. The hostel where the children stayed was beside the meeting point of the East and West Dart, a place of particular significance in many of the myths and legends associated with Dartmoor.

The group were particularly entranced with the legend of Tamara, which gave rise not only to a great deal of drama and imaginative work, but also pinpointed a real reason for writing letters with a more imaginative rather than practical content.

The quality that can be achieved in this type of work emphasises the value of returning in an ever-widening circle to the children's previous experiences in order to broaden and extend their thinking.

NAME OF THEME Dartmoor.   YEAR 6   SPIRAL
1. AUTUMN TERM 1988
2. SPRING TERM 19
3. SUMMER TERM 19

AIMS
.... To create the atmosphere and uniqueness of Dartmoor for the children.
.... To make children aware of the different aspects of Dartmoor - geological
- geographical
- aesthetic qualities of Dartmoor.
.... To instill an appreciation of the environment.
.... To instill a sense of stewardship for the environment.
.... To make them aware of the influences which determined the shaping of the landscape through change and cycles eg. seasons, weather.
.... To create the opportunities to share a series of images evoked by the moor.

RESOURCES visits, people, artefacts, community contacts, poems, stories records
Colour of landscape exhibition (october)
Pixies Holt   3rd - 7th October.
Conservation Area.
Museum loans.
A Dartmoor Church - Shaugh Prior / Lydford
Previous experience of the moor.
Crownhill Water Treatment Works.
A Marine.
Len Copley
Minibus.

OBJECTIVES
.... To enable the children to see the differences' and similarities between their environment and that of the moor.
.... To enable them to recognise distinctive features which make Dartmoor what it is.
.... To enable the children to have direct experience in caring for their own environment.
.... To enable children to appreciate the need for the care and conservation of other environments which are "unique."

CONCEPTS
Stewardship
Similarity and Difference
Cause and Effect.

EVALUATION

Fig 8.22. Dartmoor. Planning Sheet.

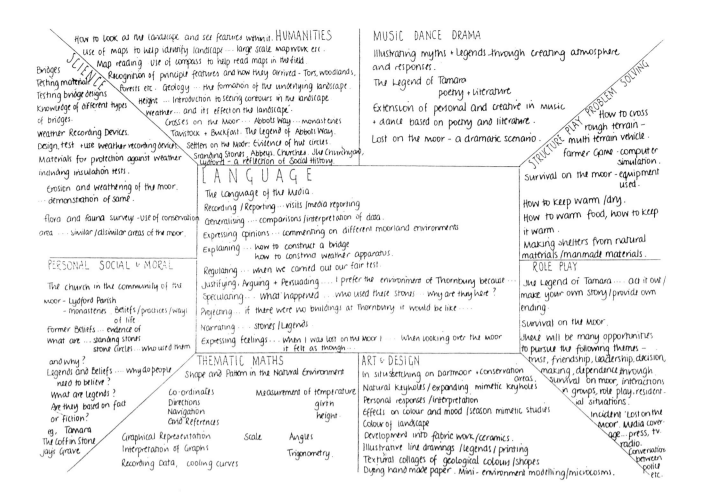

Fig 8.23. Planning Sheet.

Fig 8.24. Weekly record of work.

	Week 1	Week 2	Week 3	Week 4
STIMULUS	Visit to Bellever.	———————→	Slides, video. Review and feedback.	Pixie's Holt 'colour of Landscape'
Language Oral — Relevant vocabulary.	Reporting weather. Instruction: How to use device. Descriptive Projection Expression	———→ ←———	Reporting: sharing experiences. Expressing opinions. Imaginative in role. Justifying. explaining.	Descriptive ———→
Language Written	Recording: Note taking. Descriptive Projection Expression	———————→	Justifying explaining	Descriptive
Poetry		Group and individual responses to Bellever experience. ———————————→		———————→
Drama	Lost on the Moor. What would you do in an emergency? Group interaction, Trust, Leadership role, choices,	Communication, Interaction. ———————————→		———————→
History				
Geography	Field sketches, related map work. Land use survey. Observation of landscape. Mapreading. Observation of weather. Sites to be seen around Bellever.	follow up. ———→	Comparison of environments. Projected Maps. Research into Moorland Habitats	on site follow up. ———→
P.S.M.	'The Woodland Gospels'.	———————————————————→		
Science	Create weather recording devices. Vegetation surveys. Cookery - trad. Devon recipes. Papermaking.	Bridge material testing. Dartmoor/Con'area. Dyeing yarns with lichen etc. Multi terrain vehicles.	Bridge construction. and	Testing ———→
C.D.T. / Problem Solving	Bridges Weather recording equipment.			
Art & Design	Observing environmental patterns, shapes, form, texture. colour matching + mixing. Balance, contrast, rhythm, atmosphere, within landscape. Creating personal images in response to stimulus, combining visual + written on handmade paper.	Developed into a variety of media - fabric work, printing, ceramics,	Mimetic Invented 'keyhole' work. Weaving with dyed yarns - colour and textures of l'scape	———→
Thematic Maths	Pictorial Representation. Directions. Bearings. Compass points. Shape and Pattern.	Recording data. Measurement. ———→	Pictorial Representation. Interpretation of graphs. Recognition of regular shapes. Organised and Random Patterns.	———————→
Dance				
Music	Extension of poetry and literature work into personal creative music.			———————→

80

Fig 8.25. Weekly record of work.

	Week 5	Week 6	Week 7	Week 8
STIMULUS	Legends, myths, tales + religion drawing on experience of Pixie's Holt.	→		→
Language Oral	Evoking Images - D.Hall experience. Narrating Projection Description Expression Reporting	Narrative Imaginative ↓	Narrative. Imaginative ↓	Narrative Imaginative ↓
Language Written	Projection Description expression Imaginative - using Abbots Way; developing alternative endings.			
Poetry	Brainstorming. Group 'poetry'.		Tavy writing to Tamara. Tavy writing to Torridge. Personal love letters illustrated.	
Drama	Illustrating and Recreating Legends through drama.			
History				
Geography	Location of Crosses - Legend of the Abbots Way.	The Coffin Stones.	The Legend of Tamara - study of Tavy, Tamar + Torridge - direction, course to English Channel.	
P.S.M.	Monastic Houses of Buckfast + Tavistock. Fairs + Markets - Goosey fayre.	Lydford Church Parish.	Decision making based on personal + moral issues.	
Science	Bridges? Weather recording	Materials for protection and Insulation.	Erosion and Weathering Demonstrations. →	
C.D.T. / Problem Solving	How to survive, shelters and materials used. →		Warmth, how to keep warm, warm food. →	
Art & Design	Illustrative work. line. Designing crosses, developed	Printing illustrative designs. through printing, batik etc. →		
Thematic Maths		Cooling Curves		Pig killing tradition.
Dance				
Music	Illustrating myths and legends through creative music. Creating atmosphere + responses.		Use in Dartmoor Role Play. →	

Fig 8.26. Year 6. Dartmoor Study Sheet for use on site (pencil).

Test your pencil here:

NAME: Deborah Huxham

Fig 8.27. Year 6. Dartmoor Study.

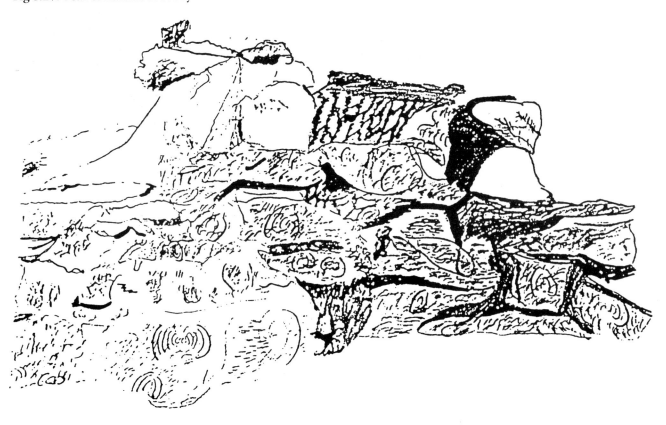

Figs 8.28 A & B. Year 6. Dartmoor Studies.

Fig 8.29. Year 6. Studies of ripples made by water (pencil).

Fig 8.30. Year 6. Water movement (batik).

Figs 8.31. & 8.32. Year 6. Illustrations for the Legend
of Tamara (micro-liner).

Figs 8.33. & 8.34. Year 6. Landscape Studies (pastel).

Figs 8.35. & 8.36. Year 6. Dartmoor Landscapes (tempera colour).

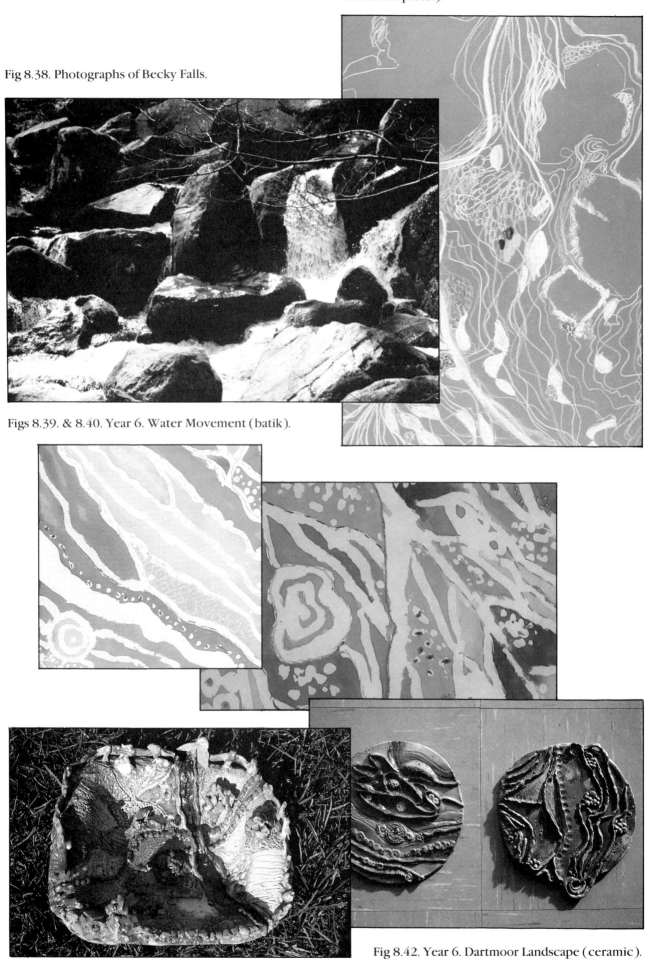

Fig 8.37. Year 6. Study of water movement (coloured chalks and pastel).

Fig 8.38. Photographs of Becky Falls.

Figs 8.39. & 8.40. Year 6. Water Movement (batik).

Fig 8.42. Year 6. Dartmoor Landscape (ceramic).

Fig 8.41. Year 6. Water Studies (ceramic).

SPRING TERM 1988

ASPECTS OF SPIRAL 2 : Fiction based projects

Years 1 and 2
'James and the Giant Peach'

Years 3 and 4
'Dragon Days'

SPIRAL 2: Fiction based project 'James and the Giant Peach'

Year groups: 1 and 2
Number of children: 129
Number of teachers: 4
Length of time: 10 weeks

This fiction based project started with the four teachers concerned building an absolutely amazing environment in the shared library resources room. They created the inside and the outside of the peach using stretched stockinet, net curtains and shades of peach fabric and paper. The intention was to heighten the children's awareness of tones and shades of colour. This was extended through a range of colour mixing activities from painting to weaving. The entrance and the exit were made incorporating two pupil tables to create a tunnel effect. The children thought 'the peach' was wonderful. They could not wait for their turn to use the role play area and creep inside the peach.

The school conservation area once again provided an environment where the children were able to study the 'real thing' – mini-beasts in situ. This in turn helped them to relate to the idea of mini-beasts inside the peach.

○ 'What were they like?'
○ 'How did they move?'
○ 'What frightened them?'
○ 'What was the world like from their angle?'

All this activity promoted detailed drawing as well as excellent oral and written language work. It was an ideal opportunity for the exploration of joints and hinges in technology. It was also planned that the children should carry out the practical technology task of making a trap to catch a mini-beast but when they came to it they were very reluctant. Proof maybe that they now empathised with those tiny creatures!

One of the most exciting aspects of the book from the children's point of view was that it had to do with magic seeds and a magic carpet. They really seemed to understand and enjoy the concept of magic and produced some really excellent magic carpet landscapes in both weaving and batik.

The excitement of the whole project spilled over into the rest of the school as other classes were invited to share their ripe 'environment'.

NAME OF THEME James and the Giant Peach YEAR 1 and 2

AIMS

To foster a love of books and gain a deeper understanding of books.

To enrich their language experience.

To encourage empathy with the characters in the book.

To heighten children's ability to listen and utilise information gained from the book.

To introduce the children to the concept of an author.

RESOURCES visits, people, artefacts, community contacts, poems, stories records

Conservation Area
Butterfly Farm.
Kitley Caves
Plymouth Airport
Visitor from Dr Barnado's or social services.
Museum Service – insects, spiders etc
Animal Man from Sparkwell.
Mountbatten Weather Station

1. Other Roald Dahl's work.
2. James and Giant Peach Music Book + Tape
3. Story Tape
4. Bad Tempered Ladybird
   V. Hungry Caterpillar
   V. Busy Spider.
   My Wonderful Aunt Stories
   * Caterpillar at Breakfast etc.

OBJECTIVES

To explore the emotions apparent in the book e.g. death, lonliness, fear etc.

To heighten their awareness of different enviroments. eg. under soil, sky, their own.

To develop their understanding of movement.

To extend knowledge of weather.

To chance their understanding of growth in relation to size.

To increase their awareness of the extended family.

CONCEPTS

Stewardship
Change and continuity
Communication

Similarity and Difference
Consensus and Conflict.
Cause and Effect.

EVALUATION

Fig 9.1. Planning Sheet

SCIENCE

HUMANITIES

Studying weather types and keeping weather records.

Looking at landscapes.

Simple mapmaking

forms of transport – boat, plane, land form.

Environments that different animals and insects live in.

Light and electricity - simple circuits

floating and sinking

flight

Water cycle and weather

Movement and forces

Structures

Met orphosis.

MUSIC DANCE DRAMA

Songs from James and the Giant Peach Music Book
Weather music - create their own.
Dance - interpretation of music from above book.
Exploring emotions + feelings apparent in the story eg. loneliness, fear, greed. excitement, floating, flying etc.

STRUCTURE PLAY-PROBLEM SOLVING

Making furniture for the peach.
Vehicle to transport peach
Make a many legged insect make it move.
Make a web, cocoon, ant hill etc.
Make a machine that will fly.
Make a weather machine.
Make a piece of weather measuring equipment.

PERSONAL SOCIAL & MORAL

Exploration of the feelings and emotions expressed in the book.
eg. fear, disappointment, selfishness, friendship, belonging, bereavement.

Stories from the World's Religions
eg. Anoxi - stories about a spider.

LANGUAGE

Recording - how and why we made the weather equipment.
Reporting - report on a visit or visitor.
Explaining - how James got into the peach.
Regulating - recipe for peach dishes eg. peach melba.
Descriptive - character sketch of James Aunts.
Justifying - why were the cloudmen so horrible to everyone?
Expressive - who was your favourite character and why?
Speculating - Would you like to live in the peach?
Comparative - Compare your family to that of James.
Creative - create a character from the poem p.39-40.

ROLE PLAY

Create the inside of the peach in the library area, with adjacent area to be the top of the peach in the sky

THEMATIC MATHS

Measurement - weight, length to standard measurement.
Time - day and night, days of the week, seasons, calendar months, o'clock, half past, quarter past / to.
Pictorial representation - pictographs, bar charts.
Volume and capacity - full and empty, half full, arbitrary units. standard units.

ART & DESIGN

Careful drawings of insects
Weaving webs
Paintings and drawings of characters in book.
Models of characters. Puppets of characters.
Making character masks for role play area
Insect prints, fruit prints
Wall hanging of scene from book, made from textures - eg. patchwork fields. furry peach etc.

Fig 9.2. Planning Sheet

89

Fig 9.3. Weekly record of work.

	Week One	Week Two	Week Three	Week Four	Week Five
STIMULUS	Title and front Cover	Chapters 1 + 2 Family	Chapters 3 - 9 Fruit + Growth	Chapters 10 - 13 Minibeasts.	Chapters 14 - 19 Moving, Journeys
Language Oral	Discussion about title and cover of book	Discussion about orphans and the extended family	Discussion and empathizing with James over loss of magic seeds	How could you catch a worm ?	Discuss the creature poem P. 39 - 40.
Language written	Speculating about the story in the book.	Describing what they think a horrible aunt would look / be like. Contrast with a nice aunt.	Expressive ... How I felt when I lost something special.	Recording ... How we tried to catch a worm.	Create a creature from the poem P. 39 - 40
Poetry	Each peach, pear, plum	Big Aunt Flo P. 20. (All the day through) What has happened to Lulu ? House on the Hill P. 106	Spike of Green P.	See Captain Beaky Poetry Book - Grasshopper, flea, spider, gnat etc.	'Dirty Beasts' by R. Dahl.
Drama	Growth of Peach.	Inside of Peach and Outside of Peach	Meeting the Creatures	Poem p. 104 - 106 Develop Characters.	→
History					
Geography		Landscapes visit to Marjons football field to view + draw from the hill.	Peaches. where do they come from , fresh and tinned	Conserving Habitats. eg. why we should not destroy minibeasts' homes.	Direction.
P.S.M.	People who care for us family.	Relationships within the family. Concept : love.	friends and their importance.	Hurt no living thing .	Anansi story Ends justifying means.
Science	Properties of paper: different types strength durability		Peaches - cookery. crumble and melba. structure of fresh peach. Soft fruit textures.	wormery characteristics of minibeasts + homes.	forces making things - move - magnets pulleys electricity
C.D.T / Problem Solving	Make a cover for the book that is durable and fits.	Make a house to go on the hill .	Box to protect a peach. Create a tree to hold a heavy weight	Make a minibeast trap (not to kill).	Make a moveable puppet eg, string puppet Make a sphere
Art & Design	Careful drawings + paintings of front cover. Portraits of James. Own front cover.	Portraits of James' Aunts, from book and their imagination. Landscapes.	Pictures and models of Magician. Inside a room or peach - models.	Careful drawings of insects. Multi-jointed mini-beasts eg, spiders.	Draw / paint the creature. Prints of creatures feet.
Thematic Maths	Measurement	Measurement	Weight	Weight	Volume and Capacity -
Dance	Growth and Expansion	Melting + Shrinking.	Animal Movements →		floating and Sinking - Peach on Sea. —
Music	Contours.				

Fig 9.4. Weekly record of work.

Week six	Week seven	Week eight	Week Nine	Week Ten	Week
Chapters 20-23 Flight	Chapters 24-29 Weather.	Chapters 30-35 Journey's End.	Chapters 36-39 The End.	Beyond the Book.	
Discuss what will happen to James and the peach in Ch·21.	Discuss what clouds could be .... eg, shapes that look like....	Discuss what will happen to them. Will they ever get back to earth?	Discuss the end of the story. Did you like it? How would you change it?	Discuss other Roald Dahl stories.	
Speculating- Write your own Ch·21.	Justifying - Why were the cloud-men so horrible to everyone?	Speculating- group stories about how they will return.	Expressing: Did you like the ending? Why? Re-write.	Creative. Write your own story along the same lines. eg. James + Giant Plum.	
→ Flying poems Monster poems.	Weather poems. (Breakthrough) Weather Rhymes+ folklore.	→ Weather Report 'wet, wet, wet' from → Rhyme Time.	'Revolting Rhymes' by Roald Dahl. →		
The Cloudmen Factory Process	→ →	Poem P.39-40 Meeting the Monsters in poems.	New York - arrival and crowd control.	→ Exploring a new place - city.	
Direction.	Weather. Make a weather station and chart the weather.	→ Weather.			
The Magic Pot concept ·greed.	'Li - ching - the rain maker'.	Easter Story. part one.	Easter story part two.	Holi, Indian festival of Spring	
→	Light / Prisms → Water Cycle → Evaporation/condensation.		Floating and sinking	Can you make things expand /shrink.	
Make a plane that will travel a distance. Make a kite. Move a heavy weight up.	Make weather measuring equipment.		Invent an object which will land a peach softly and not vertically.	Create a picture that can change when you turn it.	
Drawings of seagulls feathers.	Design the Cloudmen Weather pictures. Stuffed Clouds. Rainbows.		City skylines in watercolour and silhouettes.	Draw / Paint your new story picture.	
→	Time	→	Time	Time.	
→ Effects of Weather. →	Flight - Peach in the Air.	→ Effects of Weather.	Weather - formation of clouds, snow etc.	→ Movement of clouds, snow etc.	

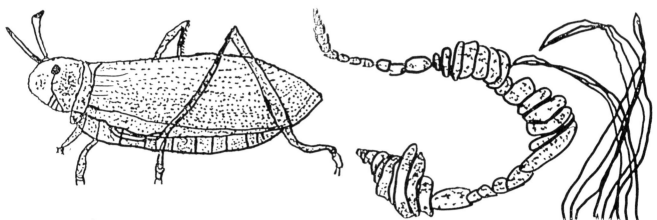

Figs 9.5. & 9.6. Year 2. Minibeasts inside the peach
(felt pen).

Fig 9.7. Year 2. Making our batiks (biro).

Fig 9.8. Year 2. Seagulls in flight (charcoal, chalk & conté).

Fig 9.9. Paper weaving in colours of the peach.

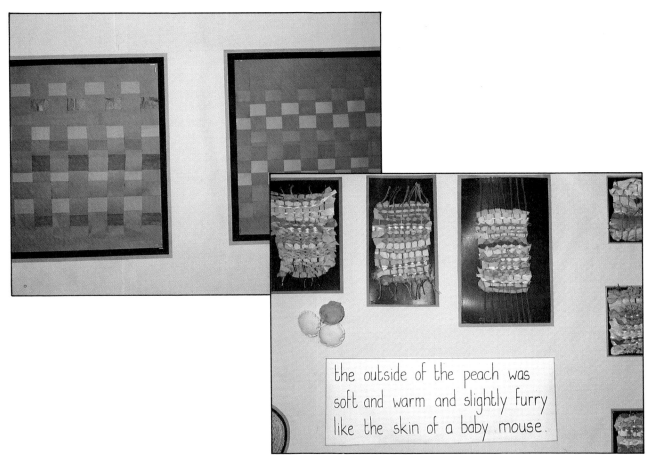

Fig 9.10. Weavings.

Fig 9.11. Peach stones. Studies and press prints.

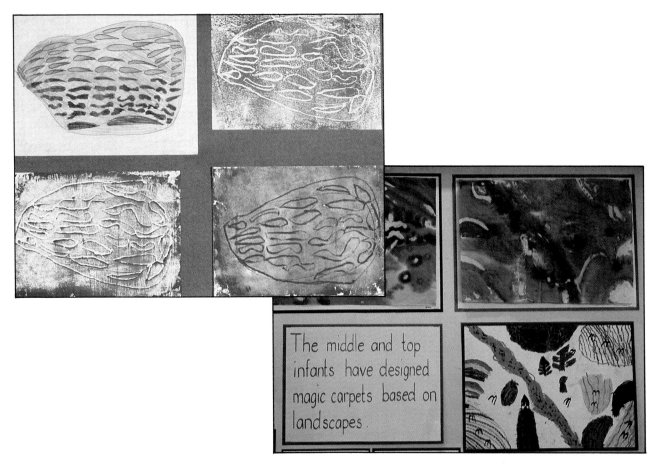

Fig 9.12. Magic carpet landscapes (batik).

SPIRAL 2: Fiction based project 'Dragon Days'

Year groups: 3 and 4
Number of children: 120
Number of teachers: 4
Length of time: 10 weeks

The team decided to look for a book that was both funny and completely fantastical and for preference they wanted it to have some historical bias. 'Dragon Days' inspired everyone as it is about down-to-earth characters involved in a total fantasy situation, with whom the children could empathise. However the staff had some doubts which they discussed in detail before they began:

○ 'Was the humour going to be too adult in its nature?'

○ 'Would the children understand that the book went back in 'time' which stood still for the duration of the story?'

○ 'The historical aspect had no supporting evidence –would the children be able to separate fact from fiction?'

Although this was a useful discussion for the four staff, none of these 'problems' actually came to light. The book was supported by a lot of 'beside the book' historical work. A time line was set up on one of the largest walls in the area. Each child contributed work to this line – 800 to 980 A.D. by looking at important events and slotting them in the appropriate place. It was stressed that King Arthur might have lived in Saxon times and they discussed what his life might have been like. Although the book provided no new evidence of King Arthur's life there was plenty of evidence about life at his supposed period in history. The Norman castle work in ceramics and analytical drawing was done on the basis that King Arthur might have lived in a castle like this. The children added information about Camelot and where it might have happened on the time line. The children became familiar with the concept that the further back in time we go the less evidence we have to support our ideas of the difference between fact, fiction and fantasy. The book provided an excellent vehicle to help children empathise with everyday situations as they are now and as they were hundreds of years ago.

The most stimulating part of the project took place when the teachers read Chapter 1 and the first part of Chapter 2 which they ended with ' … it was NOT a passage he was walking through but …'. At that point they were taken through a tunnel into the main hall which was dark and where the teachers had created a stockinet environment resembling the inside of Merlin's cave. Eerie music was played as they explored the tunnel and arrived in the cave. This experience formed the basis for some abstract work on form and structure, art, poetry, oral and written language, dance, role play and music. After two days the hall was cleared and the 'Merlin's Cave environment' was re-created in the classroom. The 'cave' was constantly used for mixing potions, making spells and creating an impetus for further imaginative work and problem solving activities.

The staff felt it was one of the best fiction based projects they had carried out, particularly in view of their earlier worries. They thought it was fun – an important element for the children which is sometimes forgotten. It also provided experience in breadth and depth that triggered the children's imaginations.

NAME OF THEME Dragon Days
by Willis Hall
YEAR 3 and 4
SPIRAL
1 AUTUMN TERM 19
2. SPRING TERM 198.
3 SUMMER TERM 19

AIMS
1. To encourage children to widen their reading experience by introducing a new author.
2. To understand the underlying concepts of the book.
3. To develop an empathy with the characters.
4. To relate the experiences in the book with those of their own.
5. To develop an understanding of conservation issues especially endangered species.
6. To develop an understanding of 'time' in relation to periods in History.
7. To introduce and develop their ability to skim and scan

RESOURCES visits, people, artefacts, community contacts, poems, stories, records

Magician – Magic circle
Books by Willis Hall
Stockinette
Medieval Costumes – Theatre Royal.
Brian Whip
Library Centre

OBJECTIVES
1. To be able to find their way around a book eg Title, author, illustrator, chapters, beginning, middle and end.
2. To be able to sequence the story or parts of it orally.
3. To be able to describe characters in detail.
4. To be able to express feelings relating to episodes in the book and in real life.
5. To be able to construct a timeline or ring drawing the main periods of history from Camelot to now.
6. To be able to identify salient points in the story.
7. To be able to understand changes in time/situation in the book.
8. To be able to argue and justify points of view.
9. To be able to use appropriately full stops and capital letters, and speech marks for more able.

CONCEPTS
Similarity and difference   Communication
Stewardship
Conflict and consensus

EVALUATION

Fig 9.13. Planning Sheet.

SCIENCE

Potions, food.
Drawbridges
Fire - roasting on spit.
Cookery - spit roast food.
Magic potions - mixing,
  designing own from book ideas.
Washing - by hand. Is it a good
method?

HUMANITIES

Geography - building up a picture of the
  landscape in story - 3D map.
Holidays - where they go, how long for, in what etc.
  - charts and graphs of info.
History - time line, change in fashion.
  Important periods of time up to now.
  Merlin, King Arthur, — the legends.
  Things we have now compared to then.
  Similarities + differences. Types of homes.

MUSIC DANCE DRAMA

Music — creating atmosphere, mood. Drum rolls, fanfares,
  trumpets, in tunnels + stockinette.
  Circus music - linking words to music.
Dance — moving through tunnels, holes.
  fear, suspicion, being followed, chased
  hiding. Association with dragons movement
  in armour... difference in weight.
Drama - Inside the box, through the tunnel
  Being chosen - under the spotlight.
  fear, suspicion of others character studies.

PROBLEM SOLVING

STRUCTURE PLAY Designing own
  tricks
  Making working
  model of drawbridge.
Castles - lego, ludoval, CDT,
  junk.
Constructing carts/cage to
transport someone/thing from
one place to another.

LANGUAGE

Reporting - Getting to the tunnel, from experience in Drama Hall.
Explaining - process of making something.
Recording - Diary of events in book.
Generalizing - about characters, period in time, holidays.
Prediction - what happens next - following cliff hanger in story.
Justifying - Merlins point of view / Arthurs point of view on hunting.
Expressing feelings - being in tunnel (darkness) fear, loneliness, injustice.
Narrating - their holidays, being chosen for something from a crowd.
Projecting to imag — through the tunnel into a chosen time. Adding a
  situations   sequel, new chapter.
Poetry - holidays, seaside, feelings from tunnel. food - medieval times.
Regulating - cooking / science experiments.
Letterwriting - in role eg. as Henry to his father. His father to manager.
formal Grammar — full stops, commas, question marks, speech marks.

PERSONAL SOCIAL & MORAL

Being chosen, feelings.
fears in tunnel.
Dragon hunt - conservation -
  endangered species.
Suspicion of things different.
Being held in dungeon.
Guilty before being convicted -
reasons for being imprisoned,
is it fair?
How do we decide
we like someone
or not?

THEMATIC MATHS

Time - periods, change / flashbacks.
Circles - everything being equal
  for all sat at round table.
    - story goes in full circle.

ART & DESIGN

Description from text - pastel, pencil.
Landscapes from description in book.
Dragons' heads - mod roc.
Models of castles
Stockinette - light / dark, shadows, colours.
fashion - costume in collage / textiles.
Armour - use of shiny materials.

ROLE PLAY

Circus - magician spotlight
on one - how do you feel?
Through the tunnel - stockinette,
tunnel in corridor to drama hall.
Merlins Cave - designed and
set up in library; bottles -
potions to mix.

Fig 9.14. Planning Sheet.

BEYOND THE BOOK

Predictions - what happens
next in chapter.
Rewriting the ending.
Adding a character - themselves
writing a chapter again in role
or from a different viewpoint
writing a sequel.
Giving chapter headings
Letter writing in role of character
Studying structure of story -
beginning, middle + end, cliff hangers
points of interest

BEFORE THE BOOK

Book covers - designed from title.
Structure of a book.
Title anagrams
Group names - make up story / book cover based on these
Using library indexes, identifying author, illustrator
  etc.
Going through tunnel into drama hall - feelings.

WITHIN THE BOOK

Character studies from book description -
  - art / language.
History related to the story. Understanding
changes in time and situation of characters
throughout the book.
Conservation issues - endangered species, hunting
Comparing book characters (of Arthur and the
Knights) with those in the legend.
Making own potions. Designing and mixing -
fair testing.
Dance / Music - moving through tunnels,
holes, being afraid, lonely.
Creating atmosphere.

'DRAGON DAYS' - Willis Hall.

NOW READ ON

The Inflatable Shop
The Last Vampire   } Willis Hall.
The Summer of the Dinosaur
Legends of Knights of the Round Table.
Dinosaurs and all that Rubbish.
Tarka the Otter
Born free
Charlie, Emma and the School Dragon.
Greensmoke, Dragon in Danger - Rosemary Manning

BEHIND THE BOOK

Role play - Merlins Cave
Visit from magician
Experience in drama hall -
  eg. dark tunnel
      stockinette
      atmosphere, music + lights
Costume day - in role.
Banquet - roasting on the spit
      circular table.

BESIDE THE BOOK

Holidays - their own experiences.
fear.
Circuses, magicians.
Clothing and fashion... now + then.
food of the time.
Castles (and homes)
General day to day differences in lifestyle.
How would children feel or react in a
similar situation?
first impressions of Henry. Importance of
first impressions. Judging people by
clothes etc.

Fig 9.15. Dragon Days. What lies behind the book?

95

	Week 1	Week 2 & 3	Week 4 & 5	Week 6	Week 7	Week 8	Week 9	Week 10
STIMULUS	Book-The Group Names Magician	Stocrinelle Tunnel: Chptr 1/2	Chptr 3 & 4	Vossidevisisto cc Chptr 5 & 6	Chptr 7/8	Man from Sparkwell Chptr 9/10	Now Read On	Banquet/Feast
Language Oral	Book structure – Title, the author etc. What makes a good book? Group names discuss if possible	Brainstorm ideas/ thoughts for being in tunnel. Stocrinelle	Character names	As written - look at passage in to	Deepening of feelings. Henry's feelings, animal nets of the dragon	Sword in the stone" – extracts looking at myth, legend/ factual about Arthur & knights	Opinions about book – evaluation. Discussion of style of book. Character into the fantasy	Oral sharing of experiences about banquet. Response to visual + aural stimuli
Language Written	Prediction from title – group names – where they go... where the group book? What might book be about?	Holidays – where children go, where they visited to... where they go to... tunnel	Character should Emily describe/ picture against Build up quotes speech marks/links	How Henry feels my mum/P.S.W. or dad, little kid. In writing. Hermit lane looking	Inrole writing as Henry + Dragon - point of view why dragons or other creatures complete the story – Henry's dilemma	Justifying reasoning point on hunting dragons or other creatures	Rewrite ending or add on end chapter or sequel sequence main part of story parts/notes	Write letter invite non king Arthur to Henry/family to the banquet
Poetry		Poetry from experience words & thoughts		Emily's impression of all around her – words to describe them				Sights/sounds/ tastes at a banquet – sensory poetry
Drama		Discussing feelings where in tunnel, where it goes? who might we meet? using suspicion. Characterise others	Suspicion – first impressions	Injustice – being different. In the dungeon. Craa in the dungeon	Hunting & conservation, two areas conflicting ideas as day passes. In story, then in present day		Preparation for banquet, role would do, now. Different roles at banquet	Banquet – in costume, taking on role of someone then – scenario
History		Description of landscape - Drawn from book p23 pictures	Time line – beginning comparisons of daily life. Then & now. Emily comes back in main periods – artefacts	Castle - different parts related to castle, banquet	Language - vocabulary discuss orally diff & similarities		Research into costumes, washing, banquets etc in preparation for	
Geography					Fortrace – building up a picture of area around Camelot	Plants – birds – eye view of Satan dark		
P.S.M.	Being chosen – how we choose why / what it feels like to be chosen		Suspicion - first impressions			As oral language		Eating etiquette – laying tables, manners, etc.
Science			Designing own potions, herbal remedies – from description in book p20-23, p42-45	Design a built castle from design in text with water drawbridge			Medieval food – menus, poems. Observation of orange. p40-41 P87-89, p90-41	Spit roasting, cooking
C.D.T. / Problem Solving		Setting up role play – Merlin's cave		washing, testing, hand washing being in the cold world		3D - Satan parts from book own	3D- Satan parts design	Design and make costume and armour
Art & Design		Build up Dragon costumed figures/ timeline Stocrinelle shadows, dark light	Large character heads made of children	Large character heads. Satan paper dragons paper dragon display village in children make chr	Drawing from description's - Dragon, knights castle. Sketch paper, printing	Fire – ache from description. Design own Satan Park for Dragons (2D or 3D)	Design own Satan Park for Dragons.	Observational drawings of each other in costume – Heraldic designs.
Thematic Maths								
Dance		Holes, tunnels, moving in Hhrough new linked to words.	Discussion of fears & suspicions move new linked to words.	Being followed, chased & hidden from description. book p31-33, P90 p92-93.	Dragon movements following description in text p.31-33, P90, 92-93. p108-111.	Characters of animals –movement & sound, brainstorm link music group with Dance group for full effect movement and music to go with it	Medieval dancing in preparation →	
Music		Brainstorm words, choice of instruments, cutting sound to	→ Research from story – adding sound effects.	Character studies. words & sounds match.			Music of banquet, make own tape for banquet →	

Fig 9.16. Weekly record of work

```
        cold shivers
         nervous scared
          dark black
             creepingfootsteps
              danksmelly
             wetdamp
            thinnarrow
              long no ending
           hard  rough
             damp wet
            shiver cold
             bumpy
           slap tap
                rain tap
             bang
                sharp.


                    Emily Addicott.
```

Fig 9.17. Year 4. Merlin's Cave (poem).

Fig 9.18. Year 4. Merlin's Cave (chalk, charcoal & pastel).

Figs 9.19. & 9.20. Year 4. Drawings of imaginary castles (micro-liner).

the arrow slites is where soldiers shot arrows and nobody could get them

the prisoners are in the dungeon

the Royal sleep in the sleeping rooms

the well is used for getting in the castle

the hall will feo

Fig 9.21. Year 4. Inside the castle (micro-liner).

Figs 9.22., 9.23. & 9.24. Year 4. Characters in the story (micro-liner).

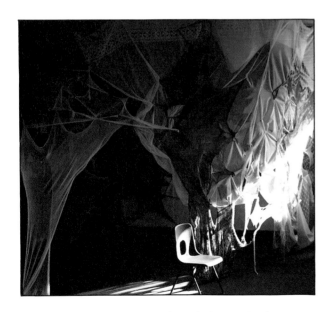

Fig 9.25. Reconstruction of Merlin's cave in drama hall.

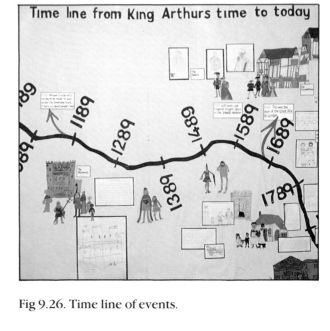

Fig 9.26. Time line of events.

Fig 9.27. Illustration for Dragon Days (tempera colour).

Fig 9.28. Dragon (ceramic).

Fig 9.29. Dragon (batik).

Fig 9.30. Dragon (batik).

SUMMER TERM 1989

ASPECTS OF SPIRAL 3

Year 5
'Man and the Sea and Man and the Land'

Year 6
Industry Based Project - 'Gardens'

SPIRAL 3:   Comparison of 'Man and The Sea' and
              'Man and The Land'

Year group: 5
Number of children: 36
Number of teachers: 2
Length of time: 5 weeks

The whole point of this project was to make the children aware of the influence different environments exert on our lives.

The children started the project by looking at black and white photographs of paintings by artists who were members of the Newlyn Group. These were photocopied and the children added colour to them. They then studied colour reproductions of the same paintings and discussed their own choice of colour compared with the artists' choices. This was followed by a great deal of work on the Newlyn artists in a variety of media culminating in individual and group ceramic models of the characters in the paintings. An interesting aspect of the work involved showing children pictures by the Newlyn artists but not their titles, and then asking them to give each picture a name and the reasons for their choice. The class went to Polperro and looked closely at the buildings around the harbour with the aim of trying to establish a set of Cornish characteristics. During the visit they worked in pairs and were asked to make a mimetic study. The issue of colour was constantly discussed and a number of colour mixing exercises took place, such as mix your own special blue colour and give it a name – there were some really imaginative ones – 'foggy blue', 'azure mist' and 'dawn light' spring to mind.

Year 5 were really inspired by the Newlyn artists. Most of them already knew the painting 'Fish Sale on a Cornish Beach' which hangs in the City Museum and they really enjoyed making both the detailed observed water colours of Polperro and their own impressions. These two approaches created an interesting basis for discussion. Part of the work involved re-enacting some of the scenes from the pictures and making a video. The final week of the project took place at Beaford – a local residential centre particularly biased towards the arts and set in the rural landscape of North Devon. Here the children were joined by an artist-in-residence – who is a painter of rural landscapes. He showed his own work to the pupils and explained his approach to landscape and the techniques he used. The children then had the opportunity to explore the landscape using a similar approach themselves.

The children also had access to the Beaford archive of photographs of all aspects of rural life in North Devon. The teachers constantly helped the children to see the similarities and differences between landscapes and seascapes. This was an invaluable in-depth experience for the children. Unlike the other themes described, there was no attempt to cover all areas of the curriculum. The work focused upon art and design and provided the children with an opportunity to work in some considerable depth and to develop their initial drawings and observations through work in a rich range of media.

The planning for this project took a different format because there was no intention to cover all areas of the curriculum – more an open ended study to compare man's sea + landscape. Obviously Maths + reading went on as usual.

COMPARATIVE STUDY:- Man and the Sea and Man & the Land

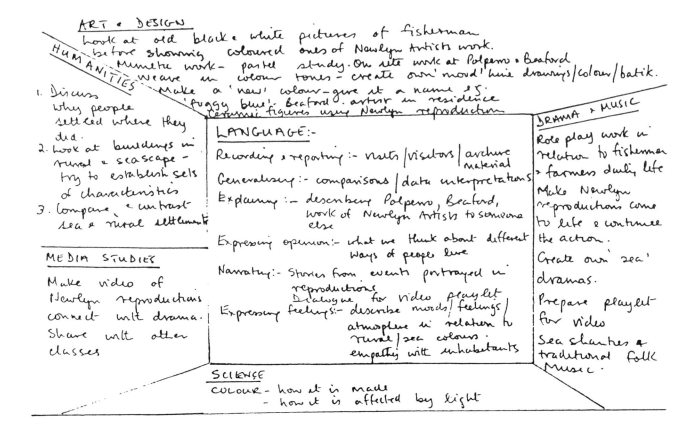

ART & DESIGN
Look at old black & white pictures of fisherman before showing coloured ones of Newlyn Artists work. Mimetic work - pastel study. On site work at Polpeno & Beaford Weave in colour tones - create own 'mood' line drawings/colour/batik. Make a 'new' colour - give it a name e.g. 'foggy blue'. Beaford. artist in residence Ceramic figures using Newlyn reproduction

HUMANITIES
1. Discuss why people settled where they did.
2. Look at buildings in rural & seascape - try to establish sets of characteristics
3. Compare & contrast sea & rural settlements

LANGUAGE:-
Recording & reporting :- visits/visitors/archive material
Generalising :- comparisons/data interpretations
Explaining :- describing Polpeno, Beaford, work of Newlyn Artists to someone else
Expressing opinion:- what we think about different ways of people live
Narrating :- Stories from events portrayed in reproductions
Dialogue for video playlet
Expressing feelings:- describe moods/feelings/atmosphere in relation to rural/sea colours. empathy with inhabitants

DRAMA & MUSIC
Role play work in relation to fisherman & farmers daily life
Make Newlyn reproductions come to life & continue the action.
Create own 'sea' dramas.
Prepare playlet for video
Sea shanties & traditional folk music.

MEDIA STUDIES
Make video of Newlyn reproductions connect with drama. Share with other classes

SCIENCE
COLOUR - how it is made
- how it is affected by light

Fig 10.1. Planning Sheet.

Summer '89 5 week module	Week 1	Week 2	Week 3	Week 4	Week 5
ORAL LANGUAGE	Establish understanding of Newlyn School through discussion of black & white photos and Newlyn colour reproductions. Discuss industries past & present	Discuss 'art' vocab. in relation to Newlyn school e.g. Colour, composition etc etc.	Discuss visit to Polpeno - difference in buildings. Importance of Sea walls. Way of life now & then Collect data	Discuss different roles in the environment	Establish understanding of rural landscape using Beaford archive. Rural industry past & present Discuss difference with sea industries
WRITTEN LANGUAGE	Write stories of Newlyn reproductions Show reproductions First without name ask children to give them a title & reasons for choice	Describe moods/feelings/atmosphere in relation to response to colour - prose and poetry	Report of visit — group response Descriptive writing of Newlyn reproduction	Write dialogue for playlet using Newlyn reproductions as basis	Justification for different environments
DRAMA	Discuss Newlyn reproductions - what do they know about fishing communities relate to previous visits to Barbican. Brainstorming to plan video playlet - what, why, how, where?	Make Newlyn reproductions come to life by continuing story of the pictures	→	Create own playlet based on Newlyn reproductions	Role play work to create empathy with farming community compare Newlyn Film 'Newlyn' dramas'
ART & DESIGN	Photocopy section to produce line drawing from Newlyn School. Photocopy own interpretation - add colour before seeing reproduction.	Mimetic studies Experience of imaginative work of Newlyn artists	Collecting info through drawing & water colour studies on site. Recreate own pictures in style of Newlyn School	→	Collect info in environment. Own interpretation of rural characters using archives Batik hedgerow study of Rural characters
	Ceramic studies of chosen characters from Newlyn School. Group ceramic				
Humanities	Relevant strands to be pulled through each week.				
Music	Sea shanties & folk music across whole project				
Media Studies	Plan & produce video across 5 week period.			FIG.10.2

Fig 10.2. Planning Sheet.

The Newlyn School'
Summer 1989.
Year 5

EXPERIENCE/ STIMULUS	MEDIA	KEY SKILL TEACHING POINTS	EXTENSION OF ACTIVITY	IMAGINATIVE ELEMENTS
visit/resource arts exp./etc.	identify medium	design/line/colour/ pattern/texture/shape/ form.	textiles/ceramics/print/ modelling/collage/ painting.	subjective activity
Reproductions of work by Newlyn artists... in particular 'The Old Pier Steps' 'The Seine Boat', 'Fish Sale' 'Off to Skibbereen' by Stanhope Forbes 'Fish Wives' by Walter Langley 'The Jack in Pilchards' by Percy Craft. photographs of character -fishermen fishwives etc. photographs of Cornish harbours, quaysides.	to follow 2D work. grey stoneware clay.	work undertaken by Wendy during Wks 1 and 2. Construction of 3D figures which portray characters within the paintings. facial expressions, stance, how he/she relates to others in scene. (a small group may concentrate on a grouping of figures) Style of clothing an important indication of occupation ie, smocks, dungerees, wellingtons, aprons etc. Shape and textures of garments. Basic skills: use of large coils and pinched forms to create basic body form Depending on position of figure problems of weight, balance, support etc. will arise.		

Fig 10.3. Planning Sheet for work in ceramics based upon Newlyn School paintings.

Fig 10.4. Year 5. Studies of Fisherman and Woman from paintings of the Newlyn School.

Fig 10.6. Study of farm worker. From drawing by Vincent van Gogh.

Fig 10.5. Study of farm worker. From photograph in Beaford Archive.

Fig 10.7. Year 5. Making studies of landscape in the grounds at the Beaford Centre in North Devon.

Fig 10.8. Year 5. Making studies of landscape in the grounds at the Beaford Centre in North Devon.

Figs 10.9. to 10.12. Year 5. Studies from paintings of
the Newlyn School.

Figs 10.13.to 10.15. Year 5. Ceramic Figures based upon Newlyn studies.

Figs 10.16. & 10.17. Year 5. Landscapes at Beaford (batik).

Figs 10.18. & 10.19. Year 5. North Devon Farmworkers (ceramic).
Based upon photographs from the Beaford Archive.

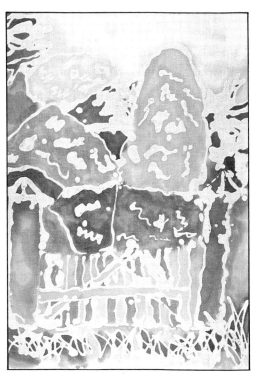

Figs 10.20. & 10.21. Year 5. Landscapes at Beaford (watercolour).

SPIRAL 3:Industry based project 'Gardens'

Year group: 6
Number of children: 107
Number of teachers: 3
Length of time: One term

The 1989 Industry project brought together all the experiences of the previous four years of working on industry based themes. The staff had learnt that structure was crucial to the success of the project but that it could inhibit the open-ended nature of the learning. It therefore seemed essential to ensure that the children should be totally involved with the teachers in developing the 'industry'. Consequently a daily evaluation took place between the children and the teachers to keep the project on target and viable.

The first stages of the planning took place in the Spring Term when the children brainstormed the possibilities and chose a name for the company that was formed. Their homework for the Easter holiday was to design a logo for 'The Lazy Daisy Company'.

The first four weeks of the project was concerned with establishing a framework for the company and included:

○ identifying hierarchies in industry;

○ choosing the company hierarchy for the firm;

○ job advertising and interviewing;

○ discussion and use of financial spread sheets — profit, loss and turnover;

○ visit to the City Council Nurseries and Parks Department

Each of the three classes focused upon one aspect of the project as their particular contribution. For example:

1. Growing, planting, mini gardens and bird feeders.
2. Garden wall planters, bulbs in boxes, cards and writing paper with a floral theme.
3. Ceramic tiles, batik cards, wrapping paper and ear rings.

The main thrust of the scheme was designing and making with the emphasis being placed upon process and quality control. The aim was to sell the products to the public at a specially organised garden party. The children carried out market research to establish how many of each of the products might sell within the local community.

The Garden Party and Sale involved a great deal of planning, all of which was undertaken by the children. They made all the party food, bunting, invitations and paper bags in the yellow and green colours of the company logo. The high spot of the day was when the eleven-year-old Chairman and Managing Director rang the local television station and they decided to interview him and his fellow directors to tell the public all about the project on the local news broadcast.

NAME OF THEME Garden Industries   YEAR 6   SPIRAL 1. AUTUMN TERM 19 2. SPRING TERM 19 3. SUMMER TERM 1989

AIMS
To give practical experience of running a small enterprise.
To develop an appreciation of
- company structure
- financial structure
- processes of production
To develop interpersonal skills.
To develop their communication skills in a variety of situations.
To develop their self awareness and their ability to present themselves in the best light.

RESOURCES visits, people, artefacts, community contacts, poems, stories, records
The Secret Garden - Frances Hodgson Burnett
Tom's Midnight Garden - Phillippa Pearce
Mundo and the Weather - Child - Joyce Dunbar
Flower Fairies
Country Diary of an Edwardian lady.
Portrait of a Country Garden.
Seed catalogues.
A variety of gardening books.

Garden Heritage Week
29th April - 2nd May
Devon Garden Festival
14th April - 3rd June

S.A.T.R.O.
Central Park Nursery.
Garden Centres.
TSW.
Plymouth Sound.
Advertising Agencies

OBJECTIVES
To enable the children to understand and appreciate the world of work.
To enable the children to organise a mini enterprise with insight.
To enable the children to work in a variety of groupings with increasing maturity, thought and logic.
To enable the children to develop and use their research skills.
To enable the children to develop a variety of communicative skills.
To enable the children to meet a variety of new situations with increased confidence.

CONCEPTS
Stewardship
Change
Cause & Effect
Similarity & Difference

EVALUATION
This project was one of the most successful industry projects that we have undertaken. We believe it was due to;
a) the pacing;
b) not over planning;
c) trying down the first 3 weeks of planning, and then letting the children dictate the pace of the project.
The project had many potential avenues for the children to explore, which was invaluable in extending their interpersonal skills.
We recommend that
a) this project is realistic in time (8 weeks),
b) it has a broad openended nature,
c) communication is crucial.

Fig 10.23. 'Lazy Daisy' Planning Sheet.

The whole project was very successful and, incidentally, made a profit of £400.00 for the school. The children gained an appreciation of the world of work and of the importance of team building in industry. Industry projects allow children to use a wide variety of skills in a range of curriculum areas and give them the opportunity to see the relevance of what is learnt in school and its connection with the world of work. This is something that every child should experience towards the end of Year 6 in the primary school, when they are mature enough to be responsible for the organisation and implementation of this kind of project.

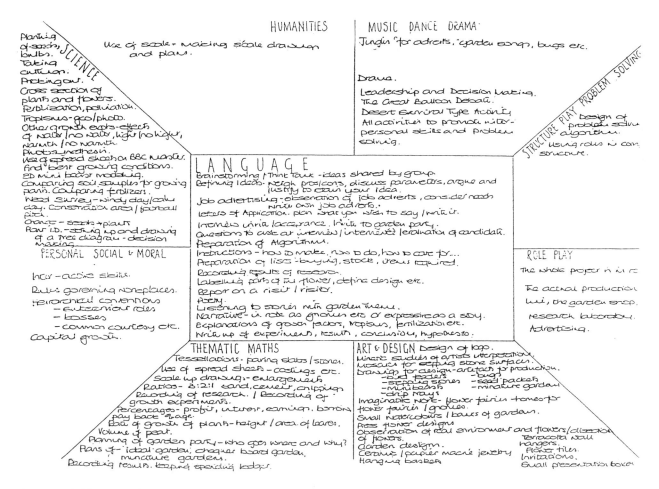

Fig 10.24. Planning Sheet.

DESIGN AND ART PLANNING   Group Name: E   Week Ending:14/4—5/5

EXPERIENCE/ STIMULUS	MEDIA	KEY SKILL TEACHING POINTS	EXTENSION OF ACTIVITY	IMAGINATIVE ELEMENTS
visit/resource arts exp./etc.	identify medium	design/line/colour/ pattern/texture/shape/ form.	textiles/ceramics/print/ modelling/collage/ painting.	subjective activity

Decoration from plant forms — Art Nouveau floral Designs 'E.Grasset'. Reproductions of work by Japanese artists celtic + medieval illustrators William Morris Photocopies. Photographs and specimens of subject matter of designs.		Main focus on the use of the shapes observed in the natural world within decorative art. Extracting a motif + stylizing. How easy is it to relate to its source? How is the design developed? Arrangement, Exaggeration, balance, flow, simplification repetition, clarity of shape etc. Importance of line — to depict shape, unify design, create flow + movement .... quality of line of importance. Texture is created by mark making although designs essentially flat.		
	pencils.	(i) Mimetic study using line of part of a selected design. (ii) observational study using line only to depict shapes and		

EXPERIENCE/ STIMULUS	MEDIA	KEY SKILL TEACHING POINTS	EXTENSION OF ACTIVITY	IMAGINATIVE ELEMENTS
visit/resource arts exp./etc.	identify medium	design/line/colour/ pattern/texture/shape/ form.	textiles/ceramics/print/ modelling/collage/ painting.	subjective activity

		patterns within a natural form eg, flowerhead, spray of leaves. (iii) Develop drawing into a 'motif' to incorporate within an 'Art Nouveau' style design — use mimetic study as a basis for layout, flow, direction etc.		
	Claywork — grey stoneware	(iv) Use of design on slabs of clay which can be assembled as 3D boxes ('planters'). Shape? Size? Skills - rolling slabs, transferring design and developing with incised and applied detail. Oxides + glazing.		

Fig 10.26. Detailed planning for 'Lazy Daisy' projects.

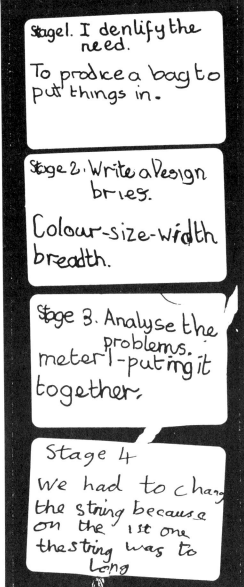

Stage1. I denlify the need.
To prodice a bag to put things in.
Stage 2. Write a Design bries.
Colour-size-width breadth.
Stage 3. Analyse the problems.
meterl-puting it together.
Stage 4
We had to chang the string because on the 1st one the string was to Long

Fig 10.27. Design process for making a 'Lazy Daisy' carrier bag.

Lazy Daisy co.
one
Lazy Daisy co.
two

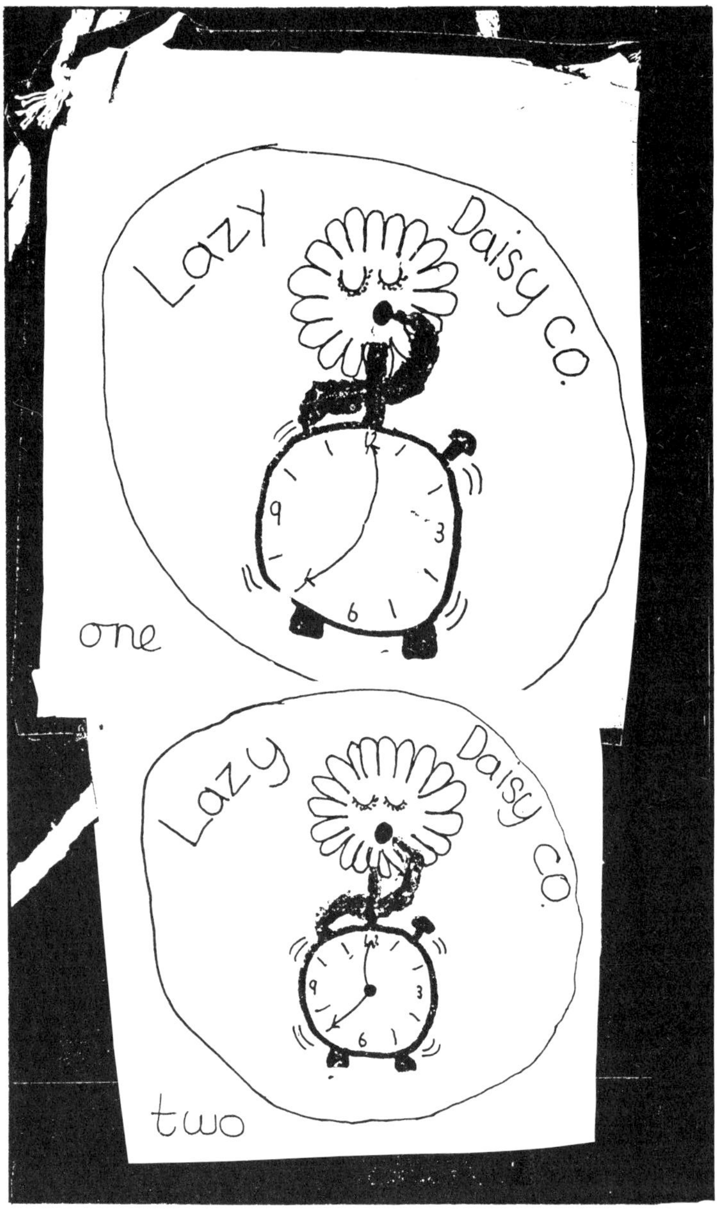

Fig 10.28. Use of company logo on carrier bags.

LAZY DAISY CO.

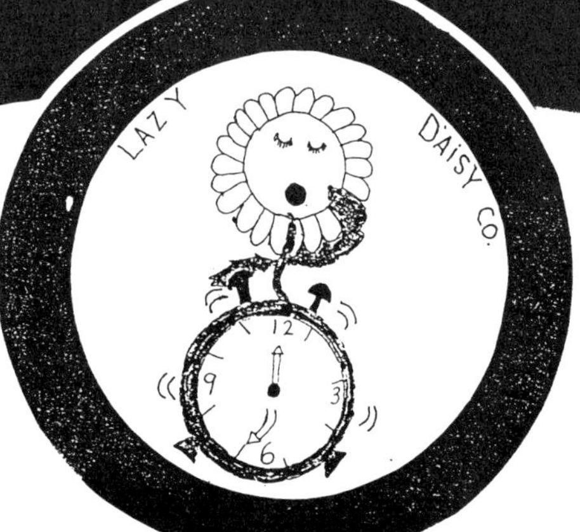

Fig 19.20. The 'Lazy Daisy' Logo.

LAZY DAISY CO.

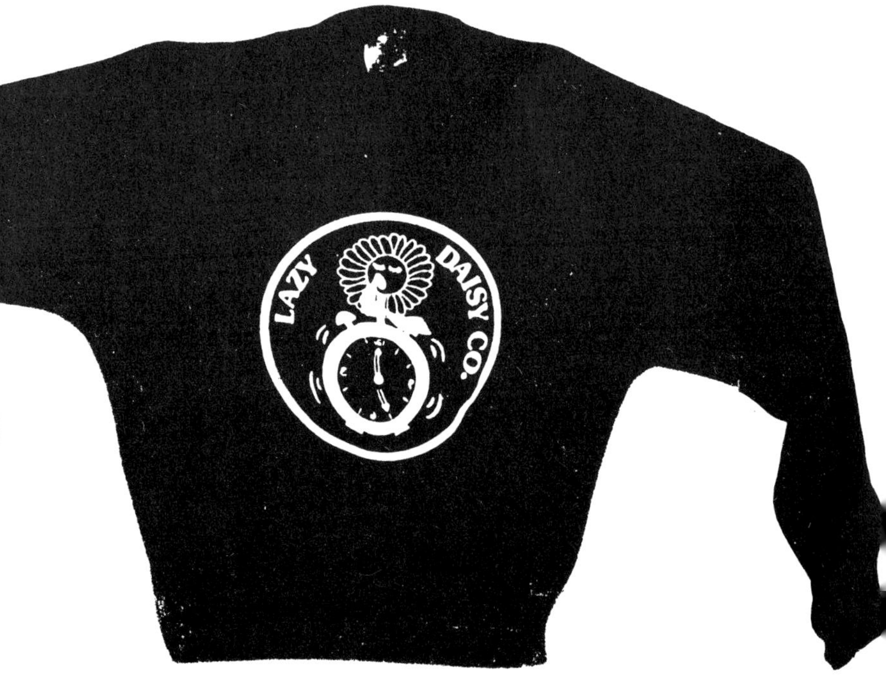

Fig 10.30. 'Lazy Daisy' T-Shirt.

Figs 10.31. & 10.32. Year 6. Children making studies from William Morris and art nouveau designs.

Fig 10.32A. Year 6. Study of Daisies (pencil).

Fig 10.33. Study from Art Nouveau Design of plant forms.

Jennifer.

Fig 10.34. Year 6. Painted Ceramic Tiles.

THE LAZY DAISY COMPANY

request the pleasure of
the company of

. . . .

at their
GARDEN PARTY AND SALE
on

FRIDAY, 30TH JUNE

at

3p.m.

R.S.V.P.

Fig 10.35. Invitation card to 'Lazy Daisy' Garden Party

Fig 10.36 & 10.37. Plant studies (micro-liner and water colour).

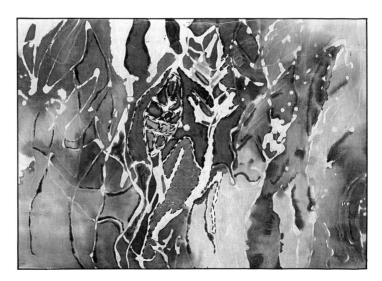

Fig 10.39. Plant Studies (batik).

Fig 10.38. Plant Studies (batik).

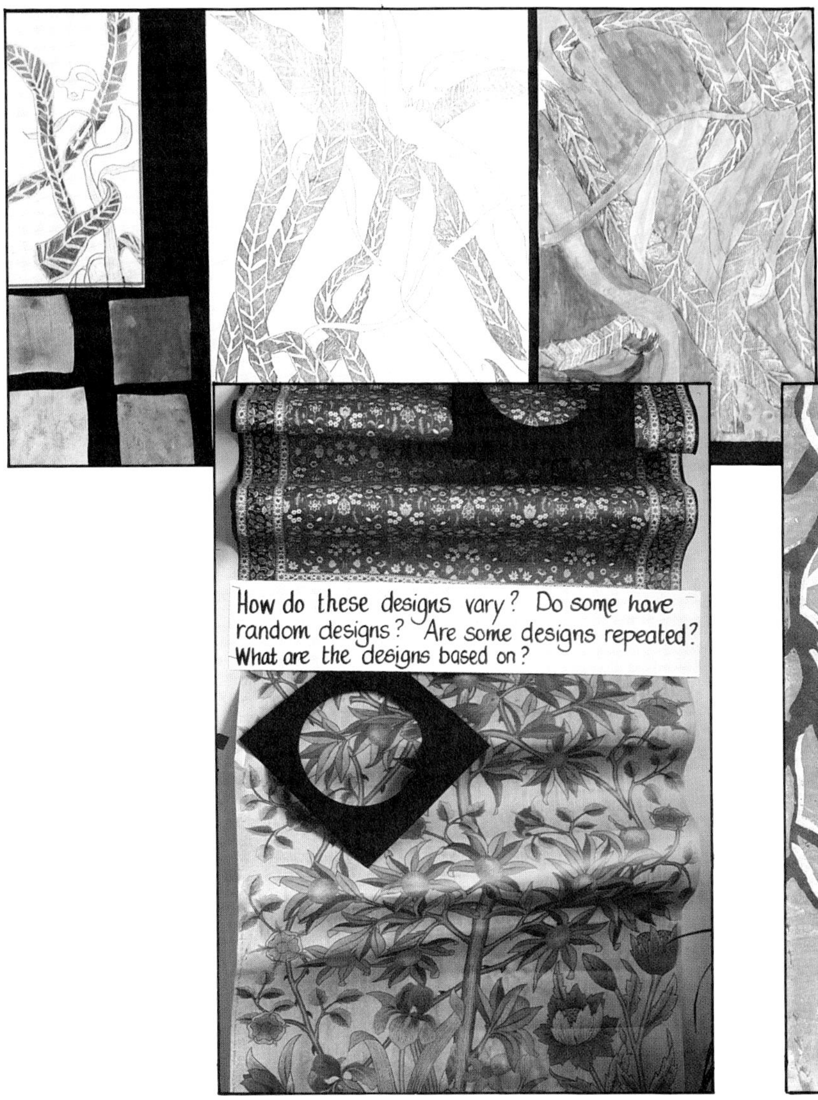

Fig 10.40. & 10.41.
Studies from natural forms and
from William Morris textiles.

How do these designs vary? Do some have
random designs? Are some designs repeated?
What are the designs based on?

Fig 10.43. Plant form. Screen print.

Fig 10.42. Daisies. Batik.

APPENDIX

Summary of Resources used to support Work in Art and Design 1988/89

VISITS AND EVENTS	WORKS OF ART	LITERATURE
Plymbridge Nursery	Calligraphy	'The Jolly Postman'
Christening	Illuminated Lettering	Traditional fairy tales – 'Cinderella',
Visit of grandparents		'The Sleeping Beauty'
Visit of mother & baby		
Wedding (links with fairy tales)		
Conservation area – school grounds		
Local park		
Wembury beach		
Mount Edgecombe		
Langley Woods		
Visit of the Animal Man		

NATURAL OBJECTS	MADE OBJECTS	PHOTOGRAPHS
Ourselves	Homes	Old Faces
Faces	Toys	Young faces
In school uniforms	Clothing from Infancy	Families
Mini beasts		
Caterpillars		
Butterflies		
Ladybirds		
Seeds		
Plants		
Flowers		
Woodland growth		
Weather study		
Autumnal colours of the natural environment		

A.1. Reception Class. Drawing from natural forms.

YEARS 1 AND 2

NATURAL OBJECTS

Parts of the body – faces, eyes, ears, hands, fingerprints

Tropical fruits

Vegetables

Plants – natural specimens from the conservation area

Fleece

Various textural objects

Fruit

Peach

Mango

Papaya

Peach stones

Stuffed seagulls

Feathers

Minibeasts

Observation of clouds and weather effects

Pieces of wood

Bark patterns

Leaves

MADE OBJECTS

Meals – Menus, Plates of various designs eg, Willow Pattern

Telephones

Teddy Bears

Musical instruments

Crisps packets

Sweet wrappers

Bottles

Mirrors, concave and convex

Lenses

Various textural objects

Peach tin labels

Clothes – favourite, old fashioned

Clothes – special occasions

Christening gowns

Wedding dresses

Uniforms

Fabrics – natural and manmade

Nylon

Velvet

Lycra

Denim etc

Of various textures patterns and colours

Costume dolls

Metal objects

Musical instruments

Xylophones

Cymbals

Glass bottles

Plastic containers

PHOTOGRAPHS

Faces – old, young

Cats' and owls' eyes

Photocopies of gloves – hands

Cloud formation and colour changes in the sky

Seagulls in flight

Aerial photographs of cities

Tree shapes

VISITS AND EVENTS

Conservation area

Plymbridge Woods

Touch Trail in conservation area

Visit by Mrs Renshaw to talk about James' blindness

A visit to College of St Mark and St John to sketch the panoramic view

Killerton House

Morwellham Quay

Copper Mine

Train and boat journeys

Resource material obtained from both visits

WORKS OF ART

Self portraits by Van Gogh, Picasso etc

Escher's optical illusion – drawing of an eye

Various landscapes from the Education Resources Service

LITERATURE

'James and the Giant Peach' by Roald Dahl

'Nini at the Carnival'

'The Iron Man' by Ted Hughes

'The Washing Line Song'

A.3. Year 1. Telephone corner

A.4. Year 2. Studies of Christening dresses.

NATURAL OBJECTS

Insects and their homes
The forest
Trees in the school ground
Patterns of bark
Children (dressed as the characters)

MADE OBJECTS

My house and its street
Patterns of bricks, slates, paving etc
Favourite rooms
Wallpapers and furnishing fabrics
Fabrics – ethnic prints, laces etc
Fashions from the Elizabethans to the present day
Religious attire
Hats
Shoes
Jewellery, etc
Suitcase

PHOTOGRAPHS

Insects and their homes
Building site, scaffolding
Windows and doors
Grandparents
Famous buildings in London
Skylines of various cities
Slides of Tower Bridge
St Pauls, Buckingham Palace etc

VISITS AND EVENTS

Cothele House – resource material obtained for subsequent use
Conservation area
Visit of an interior designer and planner
Sparkwell Wildlife Park
Visit by Irish Wolfhound
Local Church

WORKS OF ART

Various paintings of L S Lowry
Paintings featuring family life – particularly of children – Mary Cassat
Paintings of interiors – Van der Hooch, Vermeer, Frank Bramley, Gwen John, Hockney, Van Gogh ('Bedroom at Arles' – colour important to mood of room)
Paintings of Westminster Bridge by Monet, Canaletto and Whistler
'The Pool of London' by Andre Derain
Various prints of cities from Education Resource Service

LITERATURE

'Lucy and the Wolf' by Ann Jungman

City of Salford Museums & Art Gallery

A.5. 'The Cripples' (detail)
L. S. Lowry 1949

A.6. Year 3. Mimetic drawing from 'The Cripples'.

A.7. Year 3. Study of Plants in Conservation Area.

NATURAL OBJECTS

Trees

Bark

Leaves

Lichen

Moss etc

Animals

Reptiles

Birds at the Zoo

Animal and Reptile skins

Peacock feathers

Fish

Beans – observation of growth

MADE OBJECTS

The school building

The caretaker's tools

Local buildings

Derriford Hospital

Wrigley's Factory

Comprehensive School

The Church

Elm Country Centre

College of St Mark and St John

Pieces of armour – helmet, breastplate, shield

Lenses and mirrors

PHOTOGRAPHS

Animals

Reptiles

Birds

Camouflage

Flowers – Orchids

YEAR 4

VISITS AND EVENTS

Conservation area

Plymbridge Woods

The local park

College of St Mark and St John – recording sequences of movement patterns during PE and in the swimming pool

Stockinet environment of tunnels in the drama hall

Paignton Zoo

WORKS OF ART

'Children's games' by Breughel

Various paintings by Paul Klee

'Dedham Vale' by Constable

'Basin at Argenteuil' by Claude Monet

'Banks of the Seine' by Alfred Sisley

'Pont St Michel' by Marquet

Landscapes by Poussin and Breughel

Paintings featuring dragons by Ucello, Piero della Francesca

Illustrations by Arthur Rackham and Pienkowski

Heraldic designs

Abstracts by Rothko – looking at desert colours

Various jungle paintings by Henri Rousseau

Works by Van Gogh, Cezanne, Monet, Pisarro, Seurat, Klee, Matisse – looking at their uses of colour

LITERATURE

'Nature Diary' by Janet Marsh

'Country Diary of an Edwardian Lady' by Edith Holden

'Dragon Days' by Research books

A.8. Year 4. Studies of local community centre.

A.9. Year 4. Studies of figures from 'Children's Games' – Breughel.

NATURAL OBJECTS

Live and stuffed specimens of rats and mice

Natural woodland growth – leaves, bark, berries, nuts, etc

Large house plants eg, cheese plant, ferns

The Eye

Herbs

Patterns and colours of water movement

The sea

The North Devon landscape around Beaford

Trees

Grasses

Flowers, etc

Weather conditions – on the environment, on our mood, etc

Water movement – water running from tap, in a swimming pool, the river

The river surface, growth of weeds, reeds, water lilies, etc.

Inhabitants of a river – fish, pondskates, dragonflies, etc.

MADE OBJECTS

The City Centre – Old and modern buildings, shop windows, churches, statues and memorials

Buildings around Polperro Harbour looking at Cornish characteristics

Fishing vessels in the harbour – masts, sails, ropes, floats, lobster pots, fishing nets

Buildings in the local environment

Toys and games

PHOTOGRAPHS

Photographs of city centre – taken by children, in guide books and on post cards

The coat of Arms

Rats and mice

The moon

Slides of plants – enlarged as a rat's eye view

Bridges and dams

The sea

Newlyn of 100 years ago – the harbour, quayside and the people who lived and worked there

'An Artist on Every Corner' a TV film

Beaford Archive photographs of rural workers

Weather conditions

Cloud formations

Aerial views of the journey of a river

The river bank and the life around it

Television

Weather forecasts –looking at charts, symbols, patterns

Dartmouth past and present - - old prints, reference books, guide books, photographs taken by children

The fairground

VISITS and EVENTS

The City Centre

The Lord Mayor's Parlour

Railway Station

Brittany Ferries

Polperro

Residential visit to the Beaford Centre

Video interpretation of paintings through drama

River Trip to Dartmouth

WORKS OF ART

Drawings and watercolours by Chris Robinson

Work by L S Lowry and Beryl Cook

'Four Grey Sleepers' by Henry Moore; work by other war artists Nash and Sutherland

'Seaside Town in the South of France' by Paul Klee

'Venice' by Canaletto

Illuminated letters on manuscripts

Jungle paintings by Henri Rousseau – looking at large scale foliage

'The Scream' by Munch

Paintings by Max Ernst

Various modern prints from Education Resources Service

Paintings by Newlyn Artists, eg, 'The Old Pier Steps', 'The Seine Boat', Fish Sale on a Cornish Beach', 'Off to Skibbereen' – all by Stanhope Forbes

'Fishwives' by Walter Langley

'The Tuck in Pilchards' by Percy Craft

Books about the Newlyn School 'Palm Trees, Nassau' by Winslow Homer

'Water Lilies at Giverny' by Claude Monet

LITERATURE

'Rasco and Rats of Nimh' by Conly

The prologue from the Canterbury Tales – 'The Shipman'

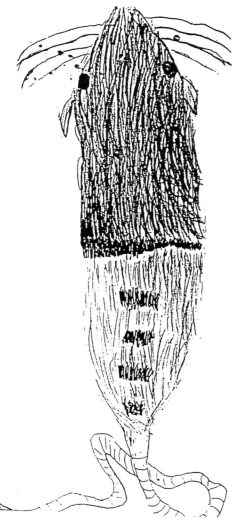

A.10. Year 5. Study of houses made on river trip to Dartmouth.

A.11. Year 5. Drawing from photograph of a rat.

NATURAL OBJECTS

The Dartmoor landscape – its vegetation, rivers, tors, etc

Bellever Forest – looking at microcosms on the forest floor, tree trunks, etc

Rivers and their surrounding areas

Live and stuffed specimens of rats and mice

Flowers, plants etc

MADE OBJECTS

Manmade divisions of the landscape, eg, walls, fences the bridge at Bellever

Flowerpots and other receptacles

Various commercial products, eg, wrapping paper

Gardens and garden designs

PHOTOGRAPHS

Photographs taken by the children during visits

Rivers

Waterfalls

Streams – photographs and slides

Flowers

Plants, etc

VISITS AND EVENTS

Bellever

Pixies holt

Conservation area

Garden centre

WORKS OF ART

'The colour of landscape' exhibition loaned by the Education Resources Service

Prints from the Elmslie Philip Collection which clearly show the shapes and divisions of the landscape

Paintings and slides showing water movement by Turner, The Impressionists, The Fauves, Abstract Artists (Gorky, Pasmore), 'Paper Pools', by David Hockney

Illustrations by Rackham and Beardsley

'Surprise', 'La Cascade' and others by Henri Rousseau

'La Joie de Vivre' and 'Evening Song' by Max Ernst

Cutouts by Henri Matisse

Surrealistic works by Salvador Dali, De Chirico, and Magritte

Floral designs by William Morris

Art Nouveau

Japanese art

LITERATURE

The Legends of Dartmoor, eg, 'Tamara', 'The Hairy Hand'

'The Secret Garden' by F Hodgson Burnett

A.12. Year 6. Making studies from William Morris & art nouveau designs

A.13. Year 6. Plant Study

NATIONAL SOCIETY FOR EDUCATION IN ART & DESIGN

TITLE	PRICE
NSEAD PUBLICATIONS	
ART, CRAFT AND DESIGN IN THE PRIMARY SCHOOL Edited by John Lancaster	£8.65
ART MACHINE Edited by Arthur Hughes, Nick Stanley and John Swift	£5.20
DEPICTIONS OF AN ODYSSEY Peter MacKarell	£11.65
GUIDE TO COURSES AND CAREERS IN ART, CRAFT AND DESIGN Tony Charlton	£12.15
NATIONAL CURRICULUM FOR ART - CURRENT ISSUES FOR CONSIDERATION Norman Binch and John Steers	£2.95
WHAT COLOUR IS THE WIND - Insights into art & visual impairment Sue Blagden and John Everett	£5.30
NSEAD/LONGMAN PUBLICATIONS	
CRITICAL STUDIES IN ART AND DESIGN EDUCATION Edited by David Thistlewood	£13.69
DRAWING, RESEARCH AND DEVELOPMENT Edited by David Thistlewood	£14.20
HISTORIES OF ART AND DESIGN EDUCATION Edited by David Thistlewood	£14.20
ISSUES IN DESIGN EDUCATION Edited by David Thistlewood	£13.69

ALL PRICES INCLUDE POSTAGE & PACKING

NSEAD The Gate House, Corsham Court, Corsham. Wiltshire SN13 0BZ
Tel (0249) 714825 Fax (0249) 716138

99   96

163199

...d ... or before

⌡96

96